WEB PROUD

THE 5-STEP ROADMAP TO FEELING PROUD OF YOUR WEBSITE AGAIN

BY

JONNY ROSS & PASCAL FINTONI

WebProud: The 5-Step Roadmap To Feeling Proud Of Your Website Again

A catalogue record for this book is available from the British Library.

ISBN 978-1-0686916-0-7 (paperback)
ISBN 978-1-0686916-1-4 (hardback)
ISBN 978-1-0686916-2-1 (ebook)

For more information and free resources visit:
www.90daymarketingmastery.com

CONTENTS

Dedication

This book is dedicated to you, the busy professional, the business visionary who pours heart and soul into crafting the perfect website, who works tirelessly to plan, design and launch the most compelling website experiences.

At times it can feel overwhelming, at other times rather lonely to be the driver of change in your business. Or, quite simply, it's not always that easy to know what to do, when, and which order. Often, what started as a fun and rewarding project has become a source of embarrassment.

Let us lighten the pressure and work with you shoulder to shoulder on this fascinating journey to make you feel proud of your website again.

Jonny Ross and Pascal Fintoni

Foreword

By Pascal Fintoni

"Sit down, I have a special project for you."

And with these simple words and this simple instruction, my career as a marketer changed forever.

The place: the London headquarters of an independent UK tour operator, or, more precisely, the office of the Managing Director. I can still conjure up to this day the sense of awe and nervousness I felt at the time.

The time: May 1994; I remember this quite vividly.

I sat down, and what followed was an animated depiction from my boss of something he excitedly called an *'Internet catalogue'*! Other portrayals that would seem clumsy to today's professionals included a computerised version of our holiday brochure, an electronic travel agency, and, by far the most creative, a dial-up travel knowledge bank.

I was then introduced to the design team, who were also sitting in the room, although I completely missed them when I first walked in (see prior reference to nerves).

The rest, as the expression goes, is history - or should that be dial-up marketing history?

I have always wondered how I became so deserving of such a significant project.

Could it be that the countless hours my siblings and I spent on the *Minitel*, the videotext online service invented by French telecoms engineer Gerard Thery in the early 1980s, finally paid off?

Perhaps I should be thankful that a few years later my dad brought home our first personal computer, the much-loved Oric Atmos, which led to numerous heated debates in the school yard as I stood my ground against hordes of ZX Spectrum and Commodore aficionados.

Maybe it had something to do with helping my colleagues find their way around Microsoft Windows 3.1 and removing the invasive AOL Internet browser from their machines whilst extolling the virtues of Yahoo or CompuServe ad infinitum?

Or was it simply a case of being at the right place, at the right time?

Either way, I remain extremely grateful for that first website project, as the positive impact it had on my personal and professional life is beyond measure.

There are other key moments and encounters that had a great influence on my journey as a digital marketing and website design professional. Too many to mention, so let me share with you a very short selection.

Let's begin with the most important event of all. On 30th April 1993, the World Wide Web project was launched by English computer scientist Tim Berners-Lee while he was working at CERN in Geneva.

I agree that the timeline of the Internet and its associated technologies might be difficult to remember, except for technology historians and quiz enthusiasts; however, the impact and incalculable benefits of being online and accessing the world's information is undeniable.

Within moments, a whole new generation of website designers and website managers was born and they have been working tirelessly together ever since - with varying degrees of success, it is fair to say - driving forward a new age for business: the age of information.

Not quite. This is in fact the age of verification, not just information, whereby the customer has been empowered to check out and verify your details to a degree that would have made spies from the Cold War green with envy.

And the go-to destination for the online consumer is a company's website. It is true that they may also access details on social networks, online directories and other sources but, ultimately, all digital roads lead to your website.

There are three more events I would like to mention, although I am mightily aware that they do not merit being chronicled in the annals of tech history or mentioned alongside the invention of the Internet. Still, these events are significant to me.

First, my conversion from digital marketing practitioner to digital marketing trainer in the early 2000s, which led to the launch of my signature course 'How To Get More Enquiries From Your Website'.

The launch of my own web marketing and content marketing agency in the early 2010s, an accidental transition into the world of self-employment I wish I had started much earlier.

And finally, and most importantly, meeting a certain Jonny Ross for the first time in the mid-2010s when we co-hosted a 'Get More Enquiries From Your Website' mastermind day in Leeds, UK.

After bidding farewell to all the participants, Jonny and I took a moment to reflect on the day and the many questions we answered, from practical design considerations to technical SEO and blogging tactics. I do not fully recall who said it first, but since my parents brought me up to be courteous and generous, I will happily credit Jonny for the following words:

"Have you noticed how so many people were embarrassed by their websites?"

Little did we realise that this simple reflection planted the seed to not only a long-standing friendship but also a shared desire to find a way for business owners to feel proud of their websites again - or, as we would eventually call it, to be 'WebProud'.

'WebProud', as a concept, is the acknowledgement that all website projects are motivated and fuelled by great emotions from you and from your visitors. It is also a way to confirm that the error of the past has always been to relegate the website design project to a technical endeavour as opposed to a customer service one, an absolute crime in my view.

The online customer is visiting your website with one single aim in mind: to avoid making a poor decision and choosing the wrong supplier or partner. The visit will be swift. The visit will be harsh. The visit will be decisive.

An unsuccessful visit will leave our prospective customer with a feeling of unease, doubts about some of the many unanswered questions, and confusion about the disconnect between the praise they heard out there and the lacklustre experience of going through the webpages of a bland and faceless organisation.

On the opposite side, a successful visit will fill the online customer with confidence, and doubts will be replaced with a desire to deal with you and your colleagues as they have gained a clear understanding that not only are you competent (who isn't?) but you are also caring. In other words, your approach to customer service, their number one concern, is exactly what they are looking forward to.

Remarkably, all these emotions, all these impressions and conclusions are reached without talking to you or anyone in your business.

As for you, feeling proud of your website is crucial to your current and future success. The 'WebProud' mindset will fuel your imagination and desire to create the best possible online experience, it will put an end to procrastination, and it will help you reconnect with your vision and true voice and, ultimately, attract the right customers.

Being 'WebProud' will make managing a website a much more enriching experience for all.

Intrigued? Keen to find out more? Ready to discover the untapped potential of your website? Then read on, use whatever information is useful to you and discard the rest. Do what you need to do to become 'WebProud' and showcase your products and services in a manner that is as unique as you are, in particular at a time when people are longing for meaningful human connection.

Pascal Fintoni

Foreword

by Jonny Ross

A Moment of Digital Revelation

It was the late 1990s, and the Internet was a thrilling frontier brimming with potential. Amid this digital revolution, I found myself captivated by the possibilities it held for business, communication and innovation. My journey into the world of digital marketing began with an unforgettable moment: the day I realised the power of connecting with people online. I was often found in newsgroups, forums and chatrooms, exploring the vast potential of this new medium! This revelation set me on a path that would ultimately lead to a career dedicated to helping businesses thrive in the digital landscape.

Early Fascination with Technology

My fascination with technology started early. I remember the excitement of receiving my first computer, the Amstrad 128, a game-changer that opened up a world of possibilities. These were the days of dial-up internet, when I had to tell my mum she couldn't make a phone call because I was using the telephone line. This frustrated her insanely! But for me, it was a thrilling gateway to the vast expanse of information and connectivity the Internet promised.

Another fascinating piece of technology I encountered was the ability to use VHS barcode scanning. With just a scan of a barcode in the *Radio Times*, our VHS recorder could auto-record shows, making the process seamless and almost magical. These early explorations laid the foundation for my deep understanding of technology and its potential to transform businesses. They also sparked debates over the merits of different operating systems and browsers, enriching my knowledge and fueling my passion for digital innovation.

Lessons from the Optician Business

In the early 2000s, I managed a chain of optician stores, a role that taught me invaluable lessons about customer service, business operations and relationship building. This experience underscored the importance of understanding customer needs and delivering exceptional service - principles that would later become central to my approach to digital marketing. It was during this period that I learned the value of meticulous organisation and the ability to handle high-pressure situations, skills that would prove invaluable in the fast-paced world of digital marketing.

The SEO Revelation and Challenges

My venture into the world of e-commerce began in 1999 during the dot-com boom with the launch of an online store selling sunglasses. We quickly became the biggest sunglass e-tailer in the UK, a status we knew from our significant buying power. We sourced all brands of sunglasses directly from manufacturers, including Oakley, Prada, Dior, Chanel and Ray-

Ban. The success of the store was thrilling, driven by the critical role of SEO in attracting traffic and generating sales.

However, this success was not without its challenges. A significant SEO penalty struck, causing our sales to drop dramatically, losing 40% of our turnover over an 18-month period. We wasted thousands of pounds with various SEO agencies, desperately trying to rectify the situation. Eventually, in 2004, I found an expert in New York who charged $250 per hour. In just two weeks, he fixed our SEO issues, turning the tide for our business.

This setback became a turning point, fueling my determination to master SEO and help others avoid similar pitfalls. The experience taught me that setbacks can be valuable learning opportunities and that perseverance is key to overcoming challenges. It was through these trials that I delved deeply into the intricacies of search engine optimisation, user journeys and user experience, knowledge that would later become invaluable in my digital marketing career.

Founding Fleek Marketing

In the early 2010s, I founded Fleek Marketing with a mission to help businesses navigate the complex digital landscape. Our goal was simple yet ambitious: to empower businesses to tell their stories in a way that resonated with their customers and drove meaningful engagement. Around this time, I began collaborating with Pascal Fintoni, a partnership that would prove to be incredibly fruitful. Together, we developed innovative strategies and training programmes to help businesses climb the Google ladder and enhance their online presence. Our approach was always client-focused, aiming to tell the story of how our clients' products and services made their customers' lives better.

Transition to Digital Marketing Training

Transitioning from a practitioner to a trainer was a natural progression. I launched the 'How To Climb The Google Ladder' course, sharing my expertise with a broader audience and witnessing the transformative impact of effective digital marketing. The feedback from these sessions was overwhelmingly positive, reaffirming my belief in the power of knowledge sharing and community engagement. I found immense satisfaction in helping others develop their skills and achieve their business goals, and this shift allowed me to reach even more businesses and make a larger impact.

Community Engagement and Professional Growth

Collaborations with esteemed institutions like the University of York and industry giants like Majestic, BrightonSEO and SEMRush further enriched my journey. These experiences broadened my perspective and solidified my reputation in the digital marketing community. Being named in the "42 Under 42" by *Insider* magazine was a significant milestone, a recognition of the hard work and dedication that had gone into my career. Engaging with the community through workshops, webinars and conferences allowed me to stay at the forefront of industry trends and continuously refine my strategies.

Collaborative Ventures and the Birth of 'WebProud'

One of the most rewarding aspects of my career has been the opportunity to engage with the community and contribute to its growth. Whether through workshops, webinars or one-on-one consultations, I've always strived to make a positive impact. The collaborative events with Pascal revealed a recurring theme: many business owners felt embarrassed by their websites. This realisation led us to conceptualise 'WebProud', a philosophy centred around creating websites that reflect a business's values, commitment to customers and brand identity. We recognised that a website is often the first point of contact with potential customers, and it should leave a lasting impression.

The Importance of a Strong Online Presence

In today's digital age, a strong online presence is more critical than ever. Customers are discerning and have a keen eye for quality. A well-crafted website instils confidence, transforms visitors into loyal customers and sets the stage for long-term success. The 'WebProud' philosophy is about more than just aesthetics; it's about embodying the essence of your business and showcasing it proudly to the world. It's about creating an online experience that is both engaging and authentic, ensuring that every interaction with your website reflects the values and quality of your business.

Embracing the 'WebProud' Philosophy

Embracing the 'WebProud' mindset means recognising the potential of your website as a powerful marketing tool. It's about overcoming procrastination, igniting creativity, and attracting the right customers. It's about feeling a sense of pride in your digital presence and knowing it accurately represents your business's mission and values. When you are 'WebProud,' you are not just creating a website; you are building a digital embodiment of your brand that can foster trust, loyalty and long-term success.

Conclusion: Unlock Your Website's Potential

As you embark on the journey outlined in this book, I encourage you to embrace the principles of 'WebProud.' Take actionable steps to improve your website, and in doing so, unlock its full potential. Let your website be a testament to your dedication, creativity and commitment to excellence. By becoming 'WebProud,' you not only enhance your online presence but also create a platform that authentically represents your business and resonates with your audience.

In conclusion, my journey in digital marketing has been driven by a passion for technology, a commitment to helping businesses grow, and an unwavering belief in the power of a strong online presence. 'WebProud' is the culmination of these experiences and insights, a roadmap to feeling proud of your website again. I invite you to join me on this journey, to harness the power of your website, and to showcase your products and services uniquely and proudly. Together, we can create a digital presence that truly reflects the best of your business.

The 'WebProud' Mindset

It all began with a simple question from a potential client: "What is your website address?"

And what followed… you know it all too well. In fact, you have experienced it all too often.

You feel the embarrassment of having to admit to yourself and others that your website is just awful, outdated, and no longer represents you, your unique proposition, your strengths and values.

You experience the disappointment of not being able to find a way to improve the performance of your website, and not being able to get yourself or your team motivated to update the site regularly.

You wish you understood how to create a better website experience for your potential clients and existing customers, and found it rewarding to manage your website using a simple yet powerful system.

We understand you might feel scared or out of your depth when it comes to online lead generation tactics. You might be dealing with teams or individuals who know more about the latest trends and technologies than you do. This can lead to a sense of disconnection and frustration, leaving you unsure of where to start or how to measure and report success effectively.

It's time to stop feeling that way about your online presence and start getting your website to work harder for you and your business or organisation.

It's time to overcome the fear and uncertainty that come with website management and embrace a clear, actionable path forward.

You may find yourself desperate for renewed motivation and clarity. You want to sell more, appear confident, and link your website performance directly with lead generation.

Your goal is to become the proud owner of a website that drives the financial success of your business or organisation, enhances your online reputation, and becomes a site others want to share and praise - a website that even your competitors will envy.

This book is your practical guide to achieving that transformation.

We will help you regain confidence in your website, understand the steps to improve it, and feel proud of your online presence once again.

With the right tools and mindset, you can turn your website into a powerful asset that represents your strengths, values and unique proposition effectively.

–

So, how do you undertake and complete that journey of transformation to feel proud of your website again?

How do you know what is going to make a real difference when faced with a multitude of advice, often contradictory and sometimes misleading?

And, practically and frankly speaking, how can we get your website to work harder for your business and make a valued contribution to your bottom line?

We think we have captured the answers to these questions and many more in this practical guide.

The content of this book is inspired by decades of delivering website masterclasses, hosting dozens of conferences a year on all things digital marketing, and the release of our 90-Day Website Mastery programme and the podcast series.

Which is why we understand fully that a website is much

more than a financial and technical investment, it is also an emotional investment. As we will mention many times, it is a direct extension of who you are as an individual and a team, an expression of your values and your passion; your website is a palpable link for your visitors to your approach to customer care.

In the true spirit of all practical guides you will have come across before, we encourage you to refer to its content regularly. This is not a 'read once and put away' book. We also invite you, indeed we fully expect you to write things down, circle interesting paragraphs, jot down your thoughts in the margins and even doodle some of your website changes - we do it all the time!

Think of your copy of 'WebProud' as your field notebook that you will claim and personalise over time.

As you quickly scan through the content of this practical guide, you will identify two clear chapters:

- **The Executive Briefings**, created to give you a strong sense of direction and to spell out the actions you will be taking soon. Use these briefings for your planning sessions, from solo work all the way to strategic meetings with your colleagues and suppliers. We sometimes refer to this chapter as the *'For Action'* segment.

- **The Bonus Section**, compiled to give you new ideas and

to stimulate your imagination. The aim is to invite you to come up with your own unique ways of crafting that all-important online experience for your visitors. We have given the chapter the *'For Inspiration'* label for obvious reasons.

Structure and a logical flow of information was an important consideration for us as consultant and educator as we planned the content of this practical guide, not to mention the genuine desire to support you in capturing your ideas in a practical action plan - which is why you will find **The Executive Briefings** both easy to follow and truly inspiring! Your next website project meeting will feel very different indeed.

Executive Briefing #1 - The Website Health Check

Executive Briefing #2 - Building Trust on Your Website

Executive Briefing #3 - Attracting the Right Website Visitors

Executive Briefing #4 - Converting Visitors into Enquiries

Executive Briefing #5: Becoming Proud of Your Website

All five briefings listed above are accompanied by suggested action plans, a series of checklists, an ideas catcher page using the dot journaling format, and, finally, two tables: one for your 'to do list' and one for your selection of 'AI solutions'. We did suggest this was more like using a field notebook!

Since your website is an extension of 'who you are and what you do', it is only natural that new ideas and follow-up questions will come to you outside of the scheduled planning sessions, from the lunchtime walk to the train journey to your next meeting, while listening to a podcast whilst at the gym, during a chance encounter with another passionate business owner and so on.

Which is why we came up with the **Bonus Section**. Sometimes we just need a little nudge in the right direction, we just want to reflect on things in a simpler way or we have a feeling that we should find inspiration differently.

All four Bonus Sections listed below have been compiled for that more casual yet very powerful way of feeling more connected with your website and its visitors:

Bonus Section #1 - *'You Ask, We Answer'* - Our answers to 10 questions about website design, content planning and more.

Bonus Section #2 - *'Website Stories'* - A series of articles and content overviews to make you think differently about website experience.

Bonus Section #3 - *'Website Engine Room'* - Our selection of 20 online solutions to improve your productivity and the performance of your website.

Bonus Section #4 - *'Website Call To Action'* - A year-long website experience roadmap! One simple change, one simple action for you to undertake each week.

So, let's put aside any regrets about what you should have done and did not do; let's ignore that unhelpful inner monologue about what you are not able to do right now.

It is time to change your mindset completely and fully embrace the journey of transformation. It is time to feel proud of your website again!

Jonny and Pascal

EXECUTIVE BRIEFING

STEP 1

YOUR WEBSITE HEALTH CHECK

Ever thought about why we all love shopping online?

It's mostly because it's super easy to find what we need, right?

But here's a fun twist: while we're all about making websites snappy and smart with the latest tech, let's not forget the real magic happens in making those human connections.

Dive into this chapter to explore how your website can do more than just function - it can connect, engage, and make people want to stay a while.

Ready to check out how healthy your website really is? Let's get started!

When it comes to the Internet, most people are using it because it's convenient. It's convenient to access information and communicate with companies – and for them to communicate with potential customers.

However, there's a risk that by focusing too much on the tech and what it can do for you, especially in terms of automation, you lose the chance to build meaningful connections. And these are essential in creating trust and positive emotions.

For that reason, we prefer to organise our Website Health Check into two key areas: ***Platform*** and ***People.***

The term *Platform* refers to the online destination you have chosen to design and manage, from simple 1-page promotional landing pages to e-commerce websites and complex information hubs.

We use the term *People* to represent your ideal website visitors, or, more precisely, the individuals who will make the decision to deal with you and purchase your products or services.

HOW TO THINK ABOUT THE PLATFORM

There are three elements to think about when it comes to the platform and the website experience:

1. Usability
2. The tech
3. Keywords and content

For example, is the site mobile friendly, and does it work well on different devices? This might seem simple, but it's really important if you want to rank higher on Google. It's also about what's on your homepage and how that displays on mobile.

If your website loads slowly, that goes against you too. Fortunately, there are some great plugins that can make it better. Make sure your images are optimised and content can be served instantly, no matter where your user is or what device they have. Your site needs to be adaptable and responsive.

When it comes to keywords, you need to be using the right words, phrases and questions that your users are looking for. To find keywords, especially long-tail keywords, there are a range of tools you can use. Google is a good place to start.

Next, think about relevancy and consistency. If you're talking about a product or service, make sure you use the keyword or name of it everywhere. That includes the title, the URL, the description and any headings. This makes it abundantly clear to search engines what the page is about, even if it's part of your pillar content (multiple pages on a topic).

Your data needs to be well-structured and easy for machines to understand, because it's the machines that display the websites and rank them. Structured data makes it easy for them to see what your website and individual pages are about and present them to people searching for that information.

For example, search Google for a lasagna recipe. You'll find the cook time, calories, images, reviews, ingredient prices and more. The data has code wrapped around the content to tell the search engine what it's about.

Google uses the data-wrapped code to mark it as frequently asked questions, or 'same as', to match it to something else. Schema searches are also really helpful. The schema allows the search engine to understand and categories your content, and link it to trusted content elsewhere, such as Wikipedia.

"YOUR DATA NEEDS TO BE WELL-STRUCTURED AND EASY FOR MACHINES TO UNDERSTAND"

Action Plan for your Platform

1. Prioritise the mobile experience. A better mobile site can give you an edge in Google searches.

2. Make sure your site loads quickly and looks good across devices. There are simple tools that can help.

3. Keep your message consistent and aligned with what your customers are searching for.

4. Embrace structured data to make your site shine in search results. It's easier than it sounds!

HOW TO THINK ABOUT PEOPLE

We believe there should be more conversations within your team, the wider business and your industry about the website. We're very aware that the spotlight is often pointed towards social media, which is no bad thing, but the website is really where the difference can be made for your business.

When it comes to people, you have to go back to relatable information. The way to do this is to consider what people are looking for and if your website delivers it. They're considering whether or not you're worthy of their time, their budget and their confidence in what you do.

There are several different things to bear in mind here, but it's worth noting that the first impression someone has of your website can have a huge impact. If you don't make it a good one, you can lose 40% of your site visitors.

If they don't feel they can trust you, you can lose another 20 to 40%. So, by the time somebody considers getting in touch with you, you've lost a lot of the conversion rate.

First Impressions

When it comes to first impressions, there are three common complaints you can use as part of your health check in addition to the platform health check.

1. "I can't easily access the information on my smartphone or tablet." This isn't just about the website being shrunk to fit a smaller screen, it's about getting to the information they need.

2. "The text and photos are old and out of date." It sounds mean, but it's quite likely the text and photos are those you used for the launch ages ago. People can tell; they can spot these things quickly. They spend so much time online that it's a skill!

3. "The navigation is confusing." The site visitor can't find what they need, the options you've given aren't clear or the language you've used is too technical or jargon heavy.

The Trust Elements

One of the biggest things people get wrong with their website is that it under-communicates with visitors. Here are six problems they might run into:

1. "I can't find any testimonials or case studies." These are vital for third-party validation, so visitors need to find them. Sometimes you do have the testimonials and case studies, but they are tucked away on a page called 'What people say about us' or similar. Make them easy to find, and make them relatable.

2. "The photos don't look real." Be careful with your visual storytelling. Pictures can cause problems because they look fake, impersonal, dated or just too small.

3. "The copy doesn't make sense." The problem here is that your website content talks only about what you do, not who you help and how you help them. You've got to bring the customer into your content and information flow.

4. “Where’s the evidence?” Are you in a regulated or professional industry, or are you making claims about your performance or impact? Then you have to back it up with evidence! You can't just say you're good at something.
The evidence can be photographic, written or a performance report carried out by a third-party authority. You may also have messages of thanks on social media, so bring these over to your website as more evidence of what you do.

5. “Your content is all about you.” The content is purely promotional and visitors don't see your passion for what you do. You don’t share industry news, evidence of you being active in your community or any helpful free content.

6. “Your contact page is boring.” You want your visitor to take action once they’ve explored your site, so you need a good call to action. If you send them to a generic contact page, they feel let down. It often doesn’t match the rest of their experience and doesn’t make it clear what happens after they’ve submitted the form.

“IT’S WORTH NOTING THAT THE FIRST IMPRESSION SOMEONE HAS OF YOUR WEBSITE CAN HAVE A HUGE IMPACT.”

Action Plan for People

1. Enhance your website user experience by simplifying navigation, offering clear options and avoiding technical jargon that may confuse visitors.

2. Provide a balanced content mix, moving beyond self-promotion by sharing information that communicates who you help and how, in addition to industry news and community involvement.

3. Strengthen trust by making testimonials and case studies easily accessible and by providing evidence to back claims, from photography to third-party authority reports.

4. Ensure the contact page matches the rest of the website's tone and provides clarity on what happens once your visitors have shared their details.

Checklist 1 from Jonny

Usability and Tech:

- When you visit your own site on your phone, does it feel as welcoming and easy as your favourite app?
- Can you recall the last time you clicked away from a slow site? How quick is yours to welcome new visitors?
- Are your website's images as quick to load as they are eye-catching, even when you're on the go?

Keywords and Content:

- What words would you type into Google if you were looking for your business? Are these words prominently featured on your site?
- Is the name of your star product or service clearly visible in the places people look first, like your headings and links?
- Think of the last article you read and loved. Was it clear and consistent? Does your website's content follow that lead?

Structured Data and SEO:

- Ever admired how some Google results have those extra helpful bits of info, like stars for reviews? Is your site set up to show off its best features in search results?
- Have you made it easy for search engines to pick out and highlight the most important information from your site?
- Is your website connected with reliable sources that give its credibility, like links to industry leaders or verified research?

Checklist 2 from Pascal

First Impressions Elements:

- When was the last time you gave your text and photos a makeover? Can you schedule regular updates of your content to keep it fresh and reflective of your current business ethos?
- Is your website navigation as easy as a walk in the park? Can you do anything to simplify the menu options and make sure everything is crystal clear without any techy talk?

Trust Elements:

- Are your testimonials and success stories relevant, recent, easy to find and reassuring?
- How can you ensure your visual storytelling is relatable, avoiding anything that feels fake, impersonal, or stuck in the past?
- Is your website content speaking directly to your customers, like a friendly conversation? Are you highlighting who you help and how, creating a friendly connection?
- Are all your claims backed up with real evidence, whether it's pictures, write-ups, or words from trusted third-party authorities?

- Is your content a mix of promotion and heartfelt sharing, like chatting with a friend? Did you check that it isn't just sales talk but also reflects your passion and community involvement, and includes helpful freebies?

Call To Action Elements:

- Is your contact page, or any other call to action webpage, more exciting than just a form? Is it an engaging part of the overall experience, letting visitors know what happens next?

PLATFORM AND PEOPLE

IDEAS CATCHER PAGE

'PLATFORM' AND 'PEOPLE' ACTION PLANNING

Tip: always start with the easier activities first and build up the complexity. Regular changes over time are always the best course of action.

What will I focus on for the next 10 days?

What will I complete in the next 30 days?

What will I achieve in the next 90 days?

'PLATORM' AND 'PEOPLE' TOOLS & AI SOLUTIONS

Complete the table below and give yourself sensible targets for the best course of action.

What do I need to do and action?

What existing website tools do I need to use more often?

What new AI solutions should I introduce and learn to use?

EXECUTIVE BRIEFING

STEP 2

BUILDING TRUST ON YOUR WEBSITE

#2

Picture this: you're having a great chat on Zoom - it's one of those calls where everything clicks, and you both hang up feeling like you've really connected.

Now, imagine if you could capture that 'Trust Moment' and share it, not just with one person but with hundreds of your website visitors?

That's what we're working on today.

We'll explore how your website can be more than just a digital space - it can be a trust-building powerhouse, turning every interaction into an opportunity to showcase your credibility and warmth.

Ready to make your website a place you're proud to share? Let's build some trust!

We're over 30 years on from the introduction of the term 'website', and it's fair to say that things have moved on (and improved) a lot in that time. The word website doesn't really do justice to the multimedia offerings people have now.

So, you need to be more specific with your language, and we need a more inspiring definition. Two things will happen when you do that. First, it creates a sense of intrigue for your audience, and they'll become curious about what you do.

Second, it helps you feel less anxious about 'running' a website and more positive about exploring the many possibilities. Adding content to it is something you can enjoy and look forward to doing.

Have you ever had a call or Teams/Zoom with someone where it goes really well for both of you? You feel you've made a connection and you each got value from the conversation? We call that the 'Trust Moment'.

But isn't it a shame that only one person got to experience that, rather than tens or hundreds of people? You came across really well and shared helpful information with them, and they enjoyed the interaction. And yet, it was missed by so many.

We need to capture those chats and share them on the website, because that's really what it's for: to record and capture the many 'Trust Moments' for those who could not be there.

Makes you think, right?

As a professional, you're constantly exploring new practices and ways of doing things. If you keep that research and new information to yourself, that's a wasted content opportunity.

Your website should be a reflection of who you are and what you're interested in. If you don't update it regularly, you're guilty of one of the biggest mistakes in website management: under-communicating.

Your audience is missing out on learning about you and what matters most to you and them. Most importantly, your future clients are looking for clear indications that you possess three important qualities and skills: common sense, communication skills and customer service.

Without these clear indications and signals, trust in your website, your business and your products and services will be much diminished.

With a strategy in place to capture and share 'Trust Moments,' it's essential to incorporate foundational elements that consistently build trust across your website. These six key elements are designed to enhance the online experience by providing clear, trustworthy information that aligns with your audience's expectations and needs.

The Six Key Elements of the Online Website Experience

1. Reviews: What are people saying? This is not just what you say people are saying, but what third parties are saying. Does that make sense?! Look for reviews about your business

on Google and other third-party websites to get a true sense of what clients think about you – and tell the world.

Think about how you can make collecting reviews part of your strategy and embed these into your website as social proof for first-time visitors.

2. Trust – via logos: This isn't necessarily about *your* logo, but about those of existing companies that inspire trust in people. For example, do you work closely with a well-known charity? Can you include their logo in the footer of your website? Similarly, if you work with a bigger business, share their logo.

Are you a member of a trade society? If you're a lawyer, you're probably a member of The Law Society. Share those logos, along with any awards or accreditations you've received from those organisations.

3. Case studies: This is about telling stories but also about sharing the impact of what you do. It communicates the 'wow factor' of an achievement. To write a really good case study, start with the problem, share the solution and then explain what the impact was. If you can share figures and statistics, that's even better.

4. Personality: People buy from people they like, whether you're working B2B or B2C. When someone is making a buying decision, the considerations are based on price and product, but also on the trust they have in the seller.

Build trust by sharing pictures of the people in your business (not stock images!). Use names, and clearly communicate the passion you have for what you do and the values you hold in everything you put out. Showcase the company culture if you're a bigger company.

5. Associates: The best type of trust is when someone else says: "You should use this organisation because they're really good." Who could be a good referrer for you? Where are these opportunities to collaborate with other companies? How can you use them to create a trust network?

6. Content: This is about passion, not just content for the sake of it. You need to believe in what you say and ensure it has real value. It's about telling stories, sharing thought pieces and the 'seven-hour rule', which is an old-school marketing technique.

What is the 'seven-hour rule'? It's about having seven hours of content so when someone visits your website, they can absorb it all and learn everything they need to know about you and your business. This can be blogs, podcasts or videos; a good mix of all three is even better.

"WHEN SOMEONE IS MAKING A BUYING DECISION, THE CONSIDERATIONS ARE BASED ON PRICE AND PRODUCT, BUT ALSO ON THE TRUST THEY HAVE IN THE SELLER."

Action Plan to Build Trust

- Implement a system for collecting and displaying updated customer testimonials and third-party reviews.
- Curate a ‘trust section’ with logos of partners, memberships and accreditations.
- Develop a series of detailed case studies that tell a story and demonstrate measurable success.
- Create an ‘Our Team’ page with real photos and bios that showcase the people behind the brand.
- Reach out to associates for cross-promotion opportunities and joint content creation.
- Assess your website’s content for the ‘seven-hour rule’ and plan for additions or enhancements to meet this threshold.

After embedding key trust-building elements into your site, it's crucial to understand the diverse needs of your visitors. This understanding will guide you in tailoring your content and features to meet the specific expectations of different visitor types, ensuring your website effectively engages and satisfies all who explore it.

What Do Your Website Visitors Want From You?

Before we get stuck into this, let's agree that the term 'visitor' is a bit vague and undefined. There are actually four different types of website visitors, so it's important to get clear on who these are, and then make sure you're giving them the information they want.

1. The Investigator: They're looking for the answer to this question: "How do you do what you do?" Are you clear about your process across your website? This isn't just on the service page, but through detailed case studies and even your FAQs page.

2. The Relationship Builder: Their question is: "Who's going to look after me?" It's the job of the 'About' and 'Meet the Team' pages to answer that, but also blogs and other content created by <u>all</u> team members.

You need to show that the passion we talked about earlier is shared and communicated by everyone in the business, not just the owner or the senior management team. After all, they'll be providing the services too.

3. The Dreamer: "What does success look like?" They're not so concerned about the process you use to get them there,

but they want to really imagine what the end result will be. Visual content is particularly good for this.

4. The Negotiator: "Why should I choose you?" is their question. They're looking for your performance message – are you making claims about the features and benefits of your offer, and do you have the evidence to back it up?

Think about these four types of visitors and what they're looking to do on your website. Which of them are making a rational, logical buying decision and who are more emotional, even intuitive? Who wants lots of detail and who prefers an overview?

We all have elements of each of these types, but there's usually a bias to one of these four. As the website owner, you do too, which means you have a blind spot about the messages you're sharing on the site.

If you're more of an Investigator, you're offering lots of detail and overlooking the sharing of the final results element that the dreamer likes. And if you're the Dreamer, perhaps you're not talking enough about your process.

"IT'S CRUCIAL TO UNDERSTAND THE DIVERSE NEEDS OF YOUR VISITORS. THIS UNDERSTANDING WILL GUIDE YOU IN TAILORING YOUR CONTENT AND FEATURES."

Action Plan to Engage Your Visitors

- Evaluate your website content to ensure clarity in explaining your process. The Investigator will check how you deliver your services and will need more than superficial statements.

- Strengthen your 'About' and 'Meet the Team' sections, and develop blogs and content that showcase the team's commitment and passion to the Relationship Builder.

- Appeal to the Dreamer by incorporating visual content that vividly portrays the desired success. Leverage images, infographics or videos to create a compelling visual representation.

- Address the Negotiator's question by emphasising performance messages. Back your claims with evidence when showcasing the features and benefits of your offer.

- Reflect on your own website biases. If you tend to be more of a Relationship Builder, ensure a balance by incorporating elements that resonate with the Negotiator, and vice versa.

Checklist 1 from Jonny

Building Trust on Your Website

Reviews:

- How can showcasing real customer feedback on your website bridge the trust gap with potential clients?
- What system will you implement to regularly collect and display fresh testimonials?

Trust via Logos:

- Which recognised partner logos or accreditations could you feature on your site to instantly signal trustworthiness?
- How can you highlight any industry awards or recognitions to bolster your credibility?

Case Studies:

- What's your most impactful client success story that demonstrates the tangible results your business delivers?
- How will you use data within your case studies to underscore the effectiveness of your solutions?

Personality:

- Are your personal and company values clearly communicated through stories and images on your site?
- What new content can you introduce to convey the passion behind your work and engage visitors on a personal level?

Associates:

- Who are your key business associates who can vouch for your credibility and how will you feature this on your site?
- What partnerships can you leverage to create a visible network of trust on your online platform?

Content:

- Does your website offer a rich mix of content that enables visitors to spend meaningful time getting to know your business?
- How can you infuse your expertise and passion into your content strategy to captivate and educate your audience?

Checklist 2 from Pascal

- How clearly does your website explain the step-by-step process of your business? Is it easy for visitors to understand? (The Investigator)
- Do your 'About' and 'Meet the Team' pages convey a genuine connection among your team members? Are they inviting and relatable? (The Relationship Builder)
- Have you used images or videos that help visitors visualise the success they can achieve with your products or services? (The Dreamer)
- When stating the features and benefits of your offerings, do you provide real evidence or examples to back up your claims? (The Negotiator)
- Can you identify the primary decision-making style of your target audience? Are they more logical, emotional, intuitive or rational?
- Consider your preferences as a business owner. Are you leaning more towards providing detailed information or showcasing the final results? Is there a balance?

- Evaluate your website content. Does it strike the right balance between offering detailed information and showcasing the end results?
- How emotionally resonant is your website? Does it connect with the intuitive aspects of your audience?
- What practical adjustments can you make to align your messaging with the diverse needs of each visitor type?
- Do you regularly draw up a simple plan for ongoing improvements to enhance trust-building elements on your website?

BUILDING TRUST ON MY WEBSITE

IDEAS CATCHER PAGE

BUILDING TRUST ON MY WEBSITE ACTION PLANNING

Tip: always start with the easier activities first and build up the complexity. Regular changes over time are always the best course of action.

What will I focus on for the next 10 days?

What will I complete in the next 30 days?

What will I achieve in the next 90 days?

BUILDING TRUST ON MY WEBSITE TOOLS & AI SOLUTIONS

Complete the table below and give yourself sensible targets for the best course of action.

What do I need to do and action?

What existing website tools do I need to use more often?

What new AI solutions should I introduce and learn to use?

EXECUTIVE BRIEFING

STEP 3

ATTRACTING THE RIGHT WEBSITE VISITORS

#3

Ever wondered how some websites seem to have all the luck drawing crowds while others get the tumbleweed treatment?

Well, it's not all luck; it's strategy. In this chapter, we're going to unlock the secrets of attracting not just any visitors, but the right ones.

Imagine combining the power of referrals with smart, easy-to-implement SEO tricks to make your website a magnet for interested parties.

Think of it as setting up a party where everyone's already interested in what you have to offer before they even walk through the door.

Let's get that traffic rolling in!

In our previous executive briefing, we explored how to build trust with your website visitors and make them feel cared for, so they're more likely to buy from you when they're ready to make a purchase or get in touch with you.

This chapter is looking into the very practical and challenging question of how to vastly increase the visibility of your website.

Put simply, you need to use the power of others.

This means a network of referrers, from both people and platforms. You're effectively piggybacking on someone else's effort in keeping in touch with your future audience.

You might actually be invited to contribute as a guest speaker to their next event, as a blogger for their website advice section or newsletter, even as an expert commentator for their next YouTube video or podcast.

Offering your time and expertise is the most effective way for individuals to make a reference to you or introduce you to people.

And of course, don't forget PR and paid promotion to complete your set of visibility activities.

As we pivot from understanding the broad strategies to enhance your website's visibility through partnerships and PR, let's narrow our focus to the very backbone of your online presence: practical SEO techniques. This section will demystify SEO, breaking it down into actionable steps that anyone can follow to improve their site's visibility and performance. We'll start with the onsite elements - those changes you can directly control on your website.

Platforms: Practical SEO Techniques

Very often, it's the basics of SEO (search engine optimisation) that are overlooked. People also worry that it's complicated, but really, it's just common sense. Ask yourself: "If I were Google, what would I do? How would I rank my website?"

It's also like traditional PR, but online. What do people say about your business, and how and where do they say it? The other key aspect is to make sure your site is accessible to the search engines so they can find it and tag your pages appropriately.

There are two sides to SEO – everything on the website itself, and everything around it, the 'offsite.' Let's consider the onsite first and use an analogy. If you were going to build a house, you'd want to make sure you've got a structural engineer, a surveyor, building regulations, planning permission and so on.

But when we build a website, we often don't think about those things. We just think about what it looks like. If it was a house, the look would come later on, after the structure has been decided.

So, it's about keywords, the content, usability, and the technical aspect. How has it been built and with what? How does the structure help it fulfil its function?

On the offsite side of things, what's going on around the world wide web? What are people saying? What are people talking about? That's all about the relevancy and links, the reviews and the reputation. Are people talking positively or negatively? And are they from trustworthy websites?

The Onsite Content

What Google likes and prioritises changes regularly, but in the last year or so its focus has been on sharing helpful content. We've also seen a rise in popularity of AI writing content for businesses; it remains to be seen whether what AI produces is valuable or not.

There's also what we call rich content, which is a variety of content. This is a mix of words, videos and images that complement each other and really work well together.

What's important is to be helpful, and there are several ways to approach this, including humour and controversy. When you think about content you'd like to produce, ask yourself: "Would I take time out of my busy working day to read or listen to or watch that content?"

Be honest. If the answer's no, you've got another question to answer. How helpful is that content?

And let's not forget about the technical side, is it usable and responsive? Will it work across different devices and browsers? What about screen size?

Have you actually tried using your website and compared it to some of the other websites that are out there? Is it easy to use and navigate? Is it responsive and has a clear call to action?

Is it fast? Humans want things to be quick, especially the younger generation. If they don't get the result they're looking for in the first couple of seconds, they move on. You want people to want to stay on your site.

Other important things to think about include:

- Consistency
- Metadata
- Headings
- Accessibility to search engines labelling content
- Structure and organisation
- Sharing relevant information

The final piece is 'what is the crowd saying?' What are people saying about your website and your business? What about things like Google reviews, social media comments and third-party review platforms?

To rank higher in the search results, these reviews help Google triangulate data about your website. Look at which sites are linking to you - how trustworthy is it? Domain authority and what Google thinks of these sites is important now.

They should be relevant to you and your industry, enabling you to build strong relationships with trusted authority organisations that are talking about you in a positive way.

"IF I WERE GOOGLE, WHAT WOULD I DO? HOW WOULD I RANK MY WEBSITE?"

Action Plan for Using Your Platform to Attract Visitors

1. Identify potential collaborators and reach out to propose partnerships, guest blogging, or other co-marketing opportunities.

2. Establish a referral programme that incentivises current clients or partners to refer new visitors to your site.

3. Conduct an SEO audit to identify and fix basic issues with website structure, content, and accessibility.

4. Regularly produce and update onsite content, aiming for a mix of text, audio, video and imagery that answers real customer questions.

5. Solicit customer feedback on the usability of your website and implement changes based on the responses.

6. Monitor and actively manage your online reputation by responding to reviews and engaging with comments on social media and review platforms.

7. Build relationships with high-authority domains for quality backlinks, enhancing your site's trustworthiness in the eyes of search engines.

People: Getting Visitors to Your Website

Unfortunately, you can't just create a website, put some content on it and hope results will happen. You have to create your own luck and encourage visitors to spend enough time on your site so that they believe in you and make that next step.

Remember that everything you do is about online reputation management.

The website doesn't exist for the sake of the content or the SEO. It should be organised so that if someone wants to check you out, they're left with a deep and positive impression of what you do, for who and how.

People will have the best understanding of you when you're passionate about what you do and the industry you operate in. Not only do you keep yourself informed, but you also take pleasure in sharing that with others.

You're curious about individuals and the impact they have on your 'ecosystem'. You make new connections and enjoy showcasing them. You're passionate about helping your customers too.

Curiosity and passion go side by side, and this is how you are getting to take full advantage of these two qualities:

You are going to conduct a 'business investigation' to help you find out more about your ideal customers.

For instance, are there others in your industry who are respected by your target audience and already have their attention?

Are your ideal customers in a membership organisation or do they attend conferences?

How do they stay informed about the industry? Which trade publications do they read?

To continue your investigation, find out who runs the tradeshow or edits the magazines they subscribe to, and create a 'who's who' of trusted individuals in your wider network.

These four groups (membership organisations, conference organisers, generic and specialist publications, trade shows) are going to be key in helping you not only to curate relevant content but also increase visibility.

The next step of your business investigation is a research project.

Become the ultimate investigator and inquire about what is already being published by those websites and authorities. Go multimedia and explore podcasts, ebooks, vlogs, infographics and more. Understand who is already in the business of communicating with your customers and creating content for them - they are your future referrers!

Once you've found that out, get into the habit of choosing a central theme or question for a particular month. Tap into your own knowledge of the industry and other key questions people have.

Three Key Tactics for Website Visibility

1. **Share The Results Of Your Investigation**: Here's an example to help you. An energy efficiency consultant chooses the theme of the impact of AI and new technologies for being more energy efficient. They decide to share, or curate, content published by any one of those four groups, along with some weekly recaps. When you do this yourself, make sure you tag the author and the brand in every repost or share of a piece of content. Often the creator will get a notification to tell them their content has been shared, and they'll thank you for doing so.

2. **Launch The Expert Q&A Series:** Once someone has thanked you, invite them to take part in an expert series. Reply as soon as you can to their message, with something along the lines of:

"You're more than welcome. It was a pleasure to share your article. In fact, I have more questions for you. Would you like to join me on my next video Q&A so we can explore and expand on the content of your article?"

The style of the original piece of content will impact the type of expert content you will produce with the creator. If they wrote a long-form article, you could ask them questions relating to it and let them share in-depth answers. If it was a quick update, perhaps a panel session with other experts is more appropriate.

Whatever you do, make sure it's published prominently on your website, and give the guest expert the link to it so they can share it on social media. But things don't end there!

3. Repurpose Your Content For More Reach: Take the conversation with you and the expert and convert it into a blog series. Transcribe the audio so you have the text to work with. An hour-long chat will give you ten pages of text, which would give you at least three or four blog posts.

Be careful: publishing it on your website won't do anything to help you increase visibility. Instead, go back to your ecosystem and offer it as a series of guest blogs. You might be published by the membership organisation or the conference organiser you identified. They publish it on their own website with a link back to your website, and they'll likely share it multiple times on their social media platforms, tagging you into each post.

And this is how you get much more visibility and traffic to your website.

Here is a final take-away for you. You're no doubt familiar with the concept of after-sales care for customers who've made a purchase from a company. Everything around visibility can be termed 'before-sales care.'

"YOU HAVE TO CREATE YOUR OWN LUCK AND ENCOURAGE VISITORS TO SPEND ENOUGH TIME ON YOUR SITE SO THAT THEY BELIEVE IN YOU AND MAKE THAT NEXT STEP."

Action Plan to Attract More Visitors to your Website

- Begin your business investigation by identifying three key industry influencers (individuals or organisations) that capture your target audience's attention.

- Find out if your ideal customers participate in membership organisations or attend conferences, and take note of the trade publications they find valuable.

- Create a simple list of individuals or entities behind trade shows, magazines and membership organisations or conferences in your industry.

- Develop a monthly habit of choosing a central theme or question related to your industry.

- Share or curate content from the identified entities, ensuring you tag authors and brands in every repost or share.

Having explored the foundational strategies for attracting the right visitors and enhancing your site's SEO, it is now time to operationalise these insights through systematic action.

In the next pages, you will find two detailed checklists. The first will guide you in implementing platform-specific visibility enhancements, while the second focuses on actively driving traffic through a focused 'business investigation' tactic.

These checklists are designed to keep you on track and ensure that every effort contributes towards building a stronger, more engaging online presence.

Checklist 1 from Jonny

Attracting the Right Website Visitors

Increasing Website Visibility - Platforms

- How can collaborating with industry influencers and platforms amplify your brand's reach and bring the right audience to your website?
- What strategies will you use to encourage referrals and mentions across different media, boosting your online presence?

Practical SEO Techniques:

- Which foundational SEO practices can you implement to make your website more appealing to search engines and users alike?
- How will you ensure your website's structure supports its functionality and visibility in search rankings?

Onsite Content Quality:

- In what ways can you incorporate rich, diverse content that provides genuine value and engages your audience on multiple levels?
- How can you utilise feedback to continuously improve the usefulness and responsiveness of your website across various devices and platforms?

Checklist 2 from Pascal

Driving Traffic - The 'Business Investigation' Tactic

- Who is currently captivating your audience, and what topics are they currently engaging in that catch the attention of your ideal customers?
- How do your ideal customers stay informed about the industry? Which trade publications do they rely on for valuable insights?
- What podcasts, ebooks, vlogs and infographics are already being published by trusted websites and authorities?
- What system will you use to record your findings and keep track of who you have contacted and when?
- How will you choose a monthly theme that aligns with your expertise? What topic could resonate with your audience?
- What content could you curate or create to spark interest? How might you express gratitude by tagging authors and brands, fostering a sense of collaboration?

- Reflect on the value of your expert Q&A. How can you repurpose this valuable content to reach a wider audience?

- Think beyond your website. Where else in your ecosystem can you offer this content? How can you leverage your growing network for increased visibility?

ATTRACTING WEBSITE VISITORS

IDEAS CATCHER PAGE

ATTRACTING WEBSITE VISITORS ACTION PLANNING

Tip: always start with the easier activities first and build up the complexity. Regular changes over time are always the best course of action.

What will I focus on for the next 10 days?

What will I complete in the next 30 days?

What will I achieve in the next 90 days?

ATTRACTING WEBSITE VISITORS TOOLS & AI SOLUTIONS

Complete the table below and give yourself sensible targets for the best course of action.

What do I need to do and action?

What existing website tools do I need to use more often?

What new AI solutions should I introduce and learn to use?

EXECUTIVE BRIEFING

STEP 4

CONVERTING VISITORS INTO ENQUIRIES

#4

Imagine your website as a buzzing marketplace, where every visitor could turn into a potential customer. Now think about what draws them in: is it the vivid display or the personable merchant?

In this session, we dive into how to make every pixel of your site not just seen but felt. We're not just filling your site with content; we're crafting experiences that engage and prompt action.

Ready to transform casual browsers into eager enquirers?

Let's explore how your website can become the ultimate conversion machine through dynamic content and strategic engagement.

We've talked already about why having the right mindset helps to have a website you can be proud of. Those who do well with their site have developed a system that is there to stimulate the imagination. For them, the running of the website is a source of positive energy; they feel re-energised as opposed to drained – it's not a chore to them.

We've also looked at why language is important, and why you need to be clear and specific with your information and content on your websites. The ideal scenario is to create a sense of intrigue for your audience, and you look forward with anticipation to creating something unique for them.

Then we're not just doing 'blogging' or website updates, but we're becoming the editor of a content series you'll explore with the reader. Imagination is what allows you to turn your everyday conversations into memorable content series.

Any interaction with a customer or colleague is an exchange of valuable information. Keeping that to yourself isn't the modern approach. Instead, capture the conversations and feature them on your website.

As we move from understanding the transformative power of having the right mindset and using precise language, let's explore practical strategies to refresh and enliven your blog and social media presence. This section delves into how you can channel your creative energies to consistently generate captivating content that not only engages but also drives enquiries. By segmenting our approach into promotional and social content, we lay a clear path towards a vibrant and dynamic online presence.

Bring New Life to Your Blog and Social Media

Tapping into your imagination means that content ideas are endless. But it's important to have the right mindset and the technique to stimulate ideas.

There are two main categories and four content types, and when you understand them, the vision is clear and you can create a monthly calendar easily.

Category 1: Promotional Content

This is designed to convert interest. Typically, by the time someone looks at promotional content and digests it, they already know a bit about you. They've probably done some due diligence to get a good idea of who you are and what you're about.

There are four types of promotional content, all designed to convert:

1. Products and services
2. Testimonials and evidence
3. Meet the team
4. Calls to action

Category 2: Social Content

This is designed to encourage people to be inquisitive about you and want to know more:

1. Industry news
2. Expert Q&A
3. Free resources
4. Company updates

By categorising them this way, you can capture these wonderful ideas into a simple matrix. It helps you to plan, be accountable, align with your strategy and make sure you're engaging with the right audience.

We suggest a three-month calendar, which you can map out in Excel, on a whiteboard or whatever online solution works best for you. The key is to simplify by breaking down the information. It helps you clarify and avoid vagueness.

Break it down by month, and then into subcategories of content type, such as promotional and social. Then you're in a position to amplify, build up and identify what you can do straight away.

Top Tip: Start with what you have and repurpose it

We're familiar with the idea of taking a big piece of content that you break into lots of different things that you use all over. In this case, though, we're talking about going back to older content and bringing it back to life. You might make it longer or change the impact it has.

There are also four types of content you'll already have:

1. Current – recent and past social media posts. What have you posted on LinkedIn, on X formerly Twitter, on Instagram? Which are the best performing blog posts* on your website?

(*Blog here actually just means any piece of content, which could be in any format).

Include content across your site here – a training session, 'Meet the Team' or an event review. Reflect on anything you've posted in the last month that could be turned into something new. You could do a monthly roundup of social media posts – the best bits.

Remember that social media moves so fast things get lost, and not everyone sees it the first-time round. You could put together an article full of the best pieces of content from X formerly Twitter, LinkedIn and Instagram. Include the original posts as screenshots. It keeps the content alive.

A good example is Amy Woods from Content 10X. What she does is 'edit up with new media elements' all of her best-performing blogs. Go back to your content and see if you can make even one small tweak. Could you change the featured image, perhaps to a photo of yourself to humanise it?

Why not record yourself reading the article to create a video or podcast to embed into the original blog post? Or, you could create a teaser trailer to tell people what a longer article's about, which you could also share on social media.

Add in some more subheadings to break down the content and turn those into visual elements that could act as a snippet and hook to draw people from social media back to the website for the full piece of content.

If you see something interesting on social media, take a screenshot and embed it into a relevant post so it's updated with newer information. If you have a 'Meet the Team' section, create some long-form content on a member of staff that brings across their personality.

People buy from people, so go beyond the usual bio sections. A day in the life interview is a good way to talk about what roles there are in your company.

Maybe you've attended and been inspired by a recent event or training session, or even a podcast you've heard. You could share the highlights and interview some of the speakers to delve into the topics of the day. It's a good way to stimulate your imagination.

"IT HELPS YOU TO PLAN, BE ACCOUNTABLE, ALIGN WITH YOUR STRATEGY"

Action Plan to Drive Engagement Through Creative Content Strategies

1. Develop a content matrix and use it to plan a three-month content calendar, incorporating both promotional and social content.
2. Audit your current and past content to identify what can be repurposed or updated.
3. Create a system for capturing daily interactions and turning them into content pieces, such as blog posts, social media updates or email newsletters.
4. Regularly review social media analytics to determine high-performing posts and use them as a basis for creating new content.
5. Experiment with different content formats, such as videos, infographics or podcasts, to add variety to your content and appeal to different audience preferences.
6. Implement a strategy for consistently refreshing your blog and social media content, ensuring it stays current and engaging.
7. Encourage team members to contribute to the content creation process, sharing their expertise and experiences.
8. Plan and execute a strategy for cross-promotion of content across various channels, utilising different content snippets and hooks to draw visitors back to the main website.

Videos to Make Your Website Work Harder

Video is Pascal's favourite type of content, because it makes what you do already have more impact. It invites you to remember to be in conversation mode, and it shows the audience that you've taken the trouble to plan, script, record and edit the video.

There are three categories of video content that work to support a business, and three content types as well. These will give you real authority in your industry.

We've said already that being curious is good for business, so to get started, you're going to get into *video curation*. You'll be finding out, on behalf of your audience, what's already out there, and sharing it with your own comments and wisdom.

Next, you move on to *video contribution,*where you are a guest on someone else's video, and then you're ready to move into creating your own videos. The first two stages help you learn a lot, which will help with the final stage: *video creation*.

Within video creation, there are three sub-categories: video messaging, video meeting and video marketing.

Video messaging is typically done on social media and are short videos that allow you to build your brand.

Video meeting is when you're the host and you have one or a panel of guests who share their expertise.

Video marketing is all about the branded content that is going to make your website work harder, and we describe three essential videos for your website in the section below.

But first, let's be more specific about the word 'video', because video content can be produced and executed in so many different ways. You might remember doodling stick figures in the corners of your school exercise book, so that when you flipped the pages it created a motion picture.

A video is, for all intents and purposes, a series of images that move along at such speed it gives the impression of motion. So it doesn't have to be an actual video; it could be still photography with animated text and music.

Maybe it's video footage with narration and text, or maybe it's you talking to the camera.

But it doesn't have to be just the talking-head style, because there are so many options. If you look on your mobile or laptop, you've probably got loads of images that could become a motion picture. Maybe this is how you should start with video marketing.

Three Essential Videos for Your Website

1. **The Welcome Video**: This is probably going to be on your homepage, and it has two functions. First, it confirms that the audience has reached the right destination, and then it summarises the key messages so the audience is intrigued and stays to consume more content.

A word of warning though: very often, the welcome video is incomplete. People sometimes forget to mention a very important thing because they're too focused on getting the sales message through.

So, we need to make sure that this welcome video follows a comprehensive story structure of: who do you help, why do you help them, and how? An example of a video that does this really well is from the UK company What3Words.
https://www.youtube.com/watch?v=vYVHzAGtJ9k

Knowing that it's hard to find business and residential addresses, even with postcodes, they've divided the world into three-metre squares and given each one a unique three-word address.

Their welcome video explains this really clearly – it sets up scenarios that the audience will have experienced, the struggle to find an address. Once they know the viewer identifies with the situation, they go into an explanation of the product itself.

You could watch the video, note down what you hear and use it as a draft script to develop your own script and storyboard. This is exactly what you want your own welcome video to look like.

2. The Personal Q&A Video: This is best suited to your blog or a landing page and is personal and sociable. If the welcome video is often incomplete, the Q&A is often overcomplicated and becomes a chore.

A good example is from Matt Cutts, answering questions about Google submitted by users from around the world. Search for it on YouTube: ***Is there a version of Google that excludes backlinks as a ranking factor?*** - the question was asked by UK agency 'Blue Bumblebee.'

It's a one-shot video, filmed on an iPhone. What makes it special is that Matt, a specialist software engineer at Google, is answering a real question from a real person. Too often, Q&A videos are created using keyword searches to find 'typical questions' people have about a product or industry, rather than a genuine request.

The question is answered simply and comprehensively and has a clear call to action.
Using Q&A videos are effective because they show you answering questions and being helpful to your audience. The production needs to be simple too.

3. The Farewell Video: This is perfect for any landing pages, including your 'Contact Us' page. This video ensures that the visitor leaves as a friend – and the way to do that is to show that you understand what it's like to be a visitor to the website of an unknown brand.

They might not feel fully confident yet about completing a purchase or booking a meeting with you, so the farewell video eliminates any last remaining doubts and helps them move to the end.

You're showing them what happens *after* they've made a purchase or made that booking. Remember, too, that this video could be a series of stills or moving images that don't show you at all – unless you want them to.

Action Plan to Boost Conversions with Targeted Video Initiatives

- Explore existing video content related to your industry and share curated videos once a week with insightful comments (video curation)
- Identify opportunities to be a guest on video series and approach two contacts per month for potential guest appearances (video contribution)
- Experiment with different video styles, from animated stills to talking heads, and record a short video introducing your business and a video answering a question (video creation)
- Develop a 30-second brand-focused video for social media and pin the message on top of your feed if the option is available (video messaging)
- Plan and host a video meeting with industry experts once a month and share valuable insights through panel discussions (video meeting)
- Plan, develop and publish on your website one of the essential videos mentioned in the chapter each month (Welcome, Q&A, Farewell)

Now, with a robust strategy for content revitalisation in place, it's essential to ensure that these efforts translate into measurable outcomes. The following checklists serve as a comprehensive guide to refine and execute your content strategies effectively. They are designed to help you systematically convert your creative content efforts into solid enquiries, ensuring that each piece of content – be it a blog post, social media update or video – works hard to engage and convert your site's visitors.

Checklist 1 from Jonny

Converting Visitors Into Enquiries

Content Mindset and Communication:

- How can you leverage everyday business interactions to create compelling content that resonates with and captures the interest of your audience?
- What unique storytelling techniques can you adopt to transform your company's narratives into engaging content series?

Blog and Social Media Revitalisation:

- What strategies can you implement to inject new life into your existing content and make it more engaging for current audiences?
- How can you utilise social media insights to inform the refresh of old content and ensure it remains relevant and appealing??

Promotional and Social Content:

- Which types of promotional content have been most effective in converting interest into enquiries, and how can you optimise them?
- How can your social content spark curiosity and lead to increased engagement and enquiries from potential customers?

Content Strategy and Planning:

- Can you describe your approach to content repurposing to maximise its reach and lifespan across different platforms?
- What system will you put in place to regularly update and align your content with current industry trends and audience interests?

Checklist 2 from Pascal

Converting Visitors Into Enquiries

Using the Power of Conversations and Video Marketing

- How can sharing existing video content in your industry provide insights and inspiration for your brand? What types of content should you focus on?
- In what ways could being a guest on someone else's video amplify your brand presence? What expert advice should you share?
- What unique aspects of your business could be highlighted through your own videos using different video styles (messaging, meetings, marketing)?
- What kind of short video messages on social media will enhance your brand visibility and help you to engage and connect with your audience?
- What is the simple way for you to host and record video meetings with industry experts to position you as thought leaders? Where on the website will you publish these?

- What key messages should your Welcome video convey to ensure your audience stays engaged? What can you learn from the What3Words example?

- How will you create a one-shot Q&A video, answering a real question from your audience in a straightforward and helpful manner? What will be the top questions?

- How can you eliminate doubts and leave a positive impression on visitors with a Farewell video? Which landing pages need a better post-purchase or post-visit experience?

CONVERTING WEBSITE VISITORS

IDEAS CATCHER PAGE

CONVERTING WEBSITE VISITORS ACTION PLANNING

Tip: always start with the easier activities first and build up the complexity. Regular changes over time are always the best course of action.

What will I focus on for the next 10 days?

What will I complete in the next 30 days?

What will I achieve in the next 90 days?

CONVERTING WEBSITE VISITORS TOOLS & AI SOLUTIONS

Complete the table below and give yourself sensible targets for the best course of action.

What do I need to do and action?

What existing website tools do I need to use more often?

What new AI solutions should I introduce and learn to use?

EXECUTIVE BRIEFING

STEP 5

BECOMING PROUD OF YOUR WEBSITE

#5

Ever hesitated before sharing your website link because it just doesn't feel quite right?

It's time to switch that feeling around. This session is all about transforming your site from just another URL to a place you're thrilled to showcase. Think of your website as your digital storefront – not only does it need to look good; it should also resonate with who you are and what you stand for.

Ready to dive into making your website a source of pride?

Let's craft a space that truly reflects your passion and connects deeply with your visitors.

Are you proud of your website, or are you embarrassed to share the link to it because you'd rather people didn't see it? Would being more consistent with updating your content make you proud of it?

Change Your Mindset

By changing your mindset, you can feel confident and in charge of your website. You want to move away from completing tasks on a to-do list and towards being the architect of an online experience.

Building trust is a recurring theme in our training sessions and throughout the 90-day website mastery programme. The website should be a convenient resource for both you and your customers, but not at the expense of meaningful human connection. Building relationships is just as important as the tech when it comes to a good website.

The purpose of a website today is to record and share your many considerations, conversations and connections. Your visitors need to feel welcomed and looked after, and that you're the person to help them. To do this, you need to engage your imagination!

The first stage is to change the language you use; be more specific in the terms you use. There's a temptation to simplify and shorten the language, but that doesn't help. It's good to think of yourself as the website editor, not the web developer.

Take everyday conversations to inspire you to put together content series, and you'll feel more excited about your website.

And of course, you can also have social content, where you offer advice rather than selling to your visitors.

With a refreshed and empowered mindset firmly in place, let's shift our focus to the tangible aspect of your website's transformation: crafting weekly and monthly content plans. This strategic approach will not only align with your renewed perspective but also set the stage for consistent and impactful content creation.

Crafting Weekly and Monthly Content Plans

We've outlined all the different types of content you should create and share, so now you need a template and a method to make it happen. Again, it's important to tap into your creative mind. This is how you demonstrate trust and encourage people to engage with you.

A good way to prepare for creating your own plan is by 'feeding' on all sorts of content that other people are putting out. That's things like industry news, competitor analysis, listening to podcasts and watching YouTube videos. When something piques your interest, make a note of it. You can refer to that list whenever you need inspiration.

An editorial plan gives you a couple of advantages. It helps you to plan, but also gives you accountability. You've agreed with yourself ahead of time the content you're going to share.

A Simple Way to Create Your Plan

Pull together a list of things and dates. That could be product launches, trade shows or events. You might not be attending these yourself, but they're relevant to your audience or your industry.

You can also keep a note of sporting events, celebrations such as Easter and Mother's Day, or anything else you're passionate about (or your clients are). Think about key milestones – your business birthday and so on.

If you're stuck, you could even have key dates in history: 'what happened on this day in YEAR'. Or refer to TV shows, particularly things like *The Apprentice*. There are also national days and weeks, such as International Women's Day on 8 March.

If you work with a charity, they might have significant dates you can talk about in your content. Finally, look out for any big competitions coming up that might be relevant to your industry, like the Booker Prize (fiction) or the Turner Prize (art).

Once you've produced your list, it becomes the basis of your editorial calendar. Use a simple spreadsheet to track the types of events down the left side, the months across the page, and then plug in your specific dates.

Spend an hour or so on this, and you'll easily find four or five content ideas per month, or one per week. The next step is to relate each of these dates to your business – which product or service do you have that you can tie in? And remember, you can create content in any format.

Have another spreadsheet that maps all this out. Include things like topic, title, industry, publishing date, keywords, call to action and anything else that is relevant to your business. Doing this ahead of time makes the content production stage much easier, because you've got a clear idea of the key elements to include.

Having established a structured and imaginative approach to content planning, it is time to put these plans into action. The following action plan will guide you through adopting the role of an online experience architect, enriching visitor interactions and ensuring your content remains engaging and interactive.

"BY CHANGING YOUR MINDSET, YOU CAN FEEL CONFIDENT AND IN CHARGE OF YOUR WEBSITE.

YOU WANT TO MOVE AWAY FROM COMPLETING TASKS ON A TO-DO LIST AND TOWARDS BEING THE ARCHITECT OF AN ONLINE EXPERIENCE."

Action Plan to Craft a Content Strategy to Elevate Your Website Experience

1. Adopt the mindset of an online experience architect to enrich the website visitor's journey and ensure that the content is engaging and interactive.
2. Craft an editorial content plan that is detailed and organised, incorporating different content types, publishing dates and strategic themes aligned with your business objectives.
3. Develop a comprehensive list of events, milestones and key dates that resonate with your business and audience, and use this to populate your editorial calendar.
4. Set aside dedicated time to brainstorm content ideas that tie in with these dates, ensuring they are aligned with your products or services.
5. Create a content template that includes all necessary elements such as topic, title, keywords, calls to action, etc., to streamline the content creation process.
6. Allocate regular hours for content inspiration activities, such as industry news analysis, competitor content review and engagement with multimedia resources.
7. Utilise a simple spreadsheet to manage your editorial calendar, keeping track of types of events, specific dates and associated content pieces.
8. Commit to reviewing and updating your content plan regularly to ensure it remains current, engaging and effective in achieving your website's objectives.

Equipped with a clear action plan to enrich your website experience, the next step involves integrating the right tools and technology. Below, we explore a selection of useful tech and apps designed to streamline your content creation process and enhance your website's functionality.

Useful Tech and Apps

1. Pexels: Photo and video site Pexels has put together a handy free calendar that has a lot of awareness days and key events you can download for inspiration.

2. Tweak Your Biz: The business site has a title generator tool that lets you find great titles for your content. Just give it your topic and a couple of keywords, and let it come up with some ideas.

It also segments the suggested titles into categories, so you could do a list post '10 Ways to do X', an advice post 'How to Master Y' or even a secret 'Crack the X Code'.

3. Days of the Year: A searchable database of all the awareness days around the world. Pop in your keyword or your job title, and it'll search for you.

4. United Nations: The UN website also has a list of international days that might be relevant to you.

5. Boords: For planning your video storyboards

6. Milanote: To organise your creative projects

7. Vlogit: Video editing app

8. InShot: Edit and enhance videos on your smartphone

9. FiLMic Pro: Cinema-quality camera for your smartphone

10. WeVideo: Video editing on the laptop

11. Filmora: Video editing on the laptop

12. Screencastify: To record your laptop screen

13. ManyCam: To help you get more from your existing tech

Recap and Action Points

Here is a quick list of the key things to think about when you start to improve and develop your website.

1. Website Health check

- Usability
- Technical aspect
- Keywords and content
- First impressions – for your visitors
- Trust elements
- Calls to action

2. Building Trust in Your Website

- Reviews
- Logos – partners, trade bodies etc.
- Case studies
- Personality
- Associates – your network
- Stories

3. **Types of Website Visitors**
   - The Investigator; The Relationship Builder; The Dreamer; The Negotiator

4. **Practical SEO Techniques**
   - Onsite and offsite
   - Third party reviews
   - Links to your site from others

5. **Referrals**
   - Guest appearances
   - Referral sites
   - Increase visibility by showing your passion
   - Reputation management – be helpful and curious about your industry

6. **Your Blog and Social Media**
   - Simplify things by breaking them down
   - Two content categories
   - Four content types
   - Create a monthly schedule

7. **Amplify by building up**
   - Start with what you have
   - Go back and repurpose up – add to existing content

8. **Videos**
   - Simplify by breaking down
   - Three categories of content
   - Three types of videos – a welcome video for the homepage, Q&A, farewell on the contact page

Your Final Checklist

Being Proud of Your Website

Mindset and Confidence:

- How does a change in mindset from task-doer to experience-architect enhance the way you approach your website's development?
- In what ways can the language and content of your website build trust and create meaningful connections with your visitors?

Content Planning and Strategy:

- What are the key elements that should be included in a weekly and monthly content plan to ensure consistency and relevance?
- How can 'feeding' on a variety of content sources contribute to the inspiration and development of your content strategy?

Editorial Calendar Development:

- What are the advantages of creating an editorial calendar, and how does it contribute to accountability and content quality?
- How can integrating various events and dates in your content plan create opportunities for engagement and relevance to your audience?

BECOMING PROUD OF MY WEBSITE

IDEAS CATCHER PAGE

BECOMING PROUD OF MY WEBSITE ACTION PLANNING

Tip: always start with the easier activities first and build up the complexity. Regular changes over time are always the best course of action.

What will I focus on for the next 10 days?

What will I complete in the next 30 days?

What will I achieve in the next 90 days?

BECOME PROUD OF YOUR WEBSITE

TOOLS & AI SOLUTIONS

Complete the table below and give yourself sensible targets for the best course of action.

What do I need to do and action?

What existing website tools do I need to use more often?

What new AI solutions should I introduce and learn to use?

CONGRATULATIONS!

You've completed all five chapters of the 'For Action' section of the Website Mastery book!

We hope you've enjoyed taking this enlightening journey through enhancing your website's presence and performance! Each chapter has equipped you with actionable strategies not only to attract the right visitors but also to engage them deeply and convert them into loyal clients.

Now, imagine the potential as you apply these insights in a systematic and practical way.

What would the next steps be? Are you ready to dive deeper?

Your journey to becoming 'WebProud' has been made clearer and a lot more interesting. Consider how much more you know and understand now about what it means to be in charge of your website.

We invite you to explore the 'For Inspiration' section of this practical guide next. It's a collection of practical answers, article reviews and tech recommendations that are sure to add to your growing bank of ideas for your next website update.

For more expansive discussions and tips, listen to the full podcast on our website.

https://90daymarketingmastery.com/

Got thoughts or a success story to share? We'd love to hear from you! Connect with us on social media and let us know how these strategies are transforming your website.

Together, let's make your digital space a beacon of success and, most importantly, an online presence and experience you can feel really proud of!

BONUS CONTENT 1

YOU ASK, WE ANSWER

'You Ask, We Answer' is the first segment of our '90-Day Website Mastery Podcast' during which we answer questions from clients and members of our community.

This bonus section contains a selection of these queries and requests for help, from myth busting to more complex technical challenges. Our replies are all always simple and practical, and we are not afraid to speak truths about the misinformation out there!

These conversations have been edited into bite-sized and easy-to-follow bulletins to give you even more inspiration about the next evolution of your website experience.

Enjoy getting answers to questions you have probably asked yourself recently.

Q: The top Google Search for 'how + website' is 'how to create a website' but the results are so misleading and inadequate, so how would you go about designing and launching a new website?

We can really understand that if you're new to it, you might be tempted to look for advice on one of the big search engines.

We agree that the information that comes up is surprisingly outdated and clearly plagiarised.

It lists the first three steps as:
1. Choose a domain name
2. Set up email addresses
3. Find a hosting company

If we're honest, that's not where we'd start at all when we're helping clients with their websites! It is sadly true that there's a lot of bad advice on Google. The other suggestions are free or low-cost templates, which may not be fit for purpose.

In our experience, choosing the domain name comes much later on. We'd start by looking at why you want a website. We'd also consider:

- What it's going to do
- Who it's going to talk to
- Who the audience is
- Who are the different stakeholders
- The purpose

- The functionality
- The desired outcome of a visit

And here is a top tip for you: by focusing on the endpoint and the content, you can then work your way backwards towards the homepage.

It is also a good idea to look for inspiration from other sectors rather than looking at competitors.

Identify elements you like and see what the current trends are in web design. Before you even choose a template, you need to take the time to reflect on what the purpose of your website is.

However, this doesn't have to be a long process, and some of these questions can be answered quite quickly. Just make sure you give some consideration to your branding and messaging and how the site will pique someone's interest, so they want to take action.

If you were preparing a presentation, you wouldn't go straight into PowerPoint to create your slides. So, with a website, we recommend getting out the Post-its and planning out the key elements. And, if possible, get someone else to help you with it, so you can talk through your ideas.

Q: What is website design?

That is a very fair question and perhaps a little harder to answer than it seems.

If you type the words 'what' + 'website' into Google, the number one question in the English-speaking world that's being asked is 'What is website design?' Unfortunately, the results are rather uninspiring and repetitive. For example: "Website design refers to the process of creating the visual appearance, layout and overall user experience of a website."

This doesn't reflect the kind of work we do, which is a lot more exciting!

For us, website design is more about: "How are you going to engage with me and make me feel welcome? How are you going to make me want to find out more when you've only got a fraction of a second to intrigue me?"

When we work with new clients, we ask them why they launched the business and where the spark comes from, and the same applies with your website. You want to get it right for your visitors, so you have to immerse yourself in the world of your customers. This means you do have to dedicate time to a research phase to capture all of that.

Think back to a conversation you've had with a prospect when you came across really well. You were impartial, passionate and told a good story. The only downside is that only the prospect heard it. So, the website is a way for you to retell this encounter and let others benefit from it too.

The function of website design has evolved over time, which is normal. Right now, a website is not a technical project. Rather, it's an extension of your approach to customer service, a way to state your values and a way to express who you are as a business entity.

Q: What is a website manager?

It's not always clear whose job it is to be the website manager or the person in charge of the online experience you wish to provide to your website visitors.

Did you know that the third most common Google search is "What are the responsibilities of a website manager?"

As with the other results we've looked at, page one of Google focuses on it being the responsibility of the IT department to look after the website, and one of their key roles is to 'make it look pretty'.

As you go further down, it gets a bit more mature, and the answers are along the lines of: "The role of the website manager is to support the business goals and to find where to support the activities of the business." This is closer to what we believe the responsibilities are.

For anyone managing the website of a larger business, they need to speak to the different departments to get a good understanding of what they do. That way, they can present solutions and options to the audience that really reflect what the company does.

As a website manager, you are ensuring that the face of that website is getting across the correct message, look, brand, tone and so on, so as soon as the visitor arrives, they know what you do.

It's your role, then, to lead a project team, with representatives from the different departments, even if there are only a couple of you taking responsibility for the website. But as the manager, it's for you to host and facilitate any meetings you have. Remember that whatever decisions you make are based on the needs of the audience.

It's a big job, because you have to install updates and check for errors and that the content is relevant. You might need to do this monthly or quarterly, but remember it's not your job to do *everything*. If something is outside your skillset, it's more than fine to get an expert in to help.

Q: What should I write in the 'About Us' section of the website?

We appreciate that the advice out there is all about sharing your values, your history and the founder stories, which seems to make sense. But if you are not careful you will end up with 'About Us' sections in your industry all sounding the same.

Instead, the 'About Us' section is like a bridge between the commercial side of the website and the social side of it (aka the blog). The 'About Us' section allows you to be creative, and it's not just about what to include, but *how* you express your story.

This is a chance to go multimedia and use photography and videos. This page is how you capture your tone of voice and what makes you unique from a customer service point of view.

The 'About Us' page can sometimes go wrong because it feels as though it is inviting you to talk about yourself, but you should flip it and put the audience first.

See it as an opportunity to show the personality of the business. It might be one of the first interactions people have with your site, so what do you want them to think and feel? It captures your tone of voice and your conversational style. And creating an 'About Us' page that's really about them shows you've thought about their needs.

Don't forget, you can be more innovative and flexible with your 'About' page, and change things if you want to. That's easier to do than it is with your product or services pages. If you get it right, it could be the start of a longer conversation.

Give people the opportunity to get to know you and remember that people buy from people. They don't want to see stock photography; they want to see you. Be conversational about yourself and bring your business to life.

This approach still allows you to share your core values but in such a way that the prospect of working with you is more appealing to visitors. You could also talk about your team in a different way.

Final tip: create a short summary on the main 'About Us' page but link it to longer biography pages. We want you to find ways to challenge your preconceptions of the 'About Us' section.

Q: How often should I blog?

Of course, being consistent with your content creation is essential, but there's no point just blogging for the sake of blogging; it's got to be worthwhile.
Have you done the research and are you certain that the content you are sharing is relevant? Is someone going to truly take five minutes out of their day to consume your content?

If you have not done the research and have some indications that what you have created is of interest, there's no point.

When it comes to content, we recommend talking about four different topics, which we've mentioned previously:

- Industry news
- Expert Q&As
- Tech news
- Company updates

Let's say you publish one of these each week, and you're therefore blogging four times a month. If you feel you can keep to that consistency, it's ideal. But you must be sure that you can stick to it!

That's why we recommend a three-month plan and having a central theme for each month. Mapping it all out first and then doing your keyword research will make it more manageable – and enjoyable!

Q: Will My Google ranking be affected if I use a website builder?

We're amazed that people still worry about using a website builder or templates (such as SquareSpace). It's not an issue at all. If you know what you're doing, or you have a skilled developer to help you, there's no limitation to what you can do.

They're coded and developed in a way that Google likes, and they can be really well-optimised.

The problem comes if you work with someone who doesn't really know how to customise the site or edit the code; that's where the templates limit you. There's also a risk that your website can look like a rush job.

Google themselves have said that they do not penalise sites created on the builder platforms (only sites with poor content!). The code is clean and the templates work well.

Where you're more likely to get caught out is with the user experience, which is why we encourage you to use a developer to help you.

Q: How do I find the right person to build my next website?

This is a question we've both been asked often and it is also the top question on forums such as Quora.

It's important to have a list of requirements for the new person. Think of them as an extended part of your team, even if they're a freelancer or from an agency. Have a scoring system so you can effectively assess each candidate.

Spend time putting together a really good, detailed brief – which means itemising what you need the website to have and asking the web developer for costs, their process and references from past clients. Get the brief right and you can use it in the selection process.

If you're just starting out, don't be afraid to go to market and say that you don't know what you want. In that case, ask the expert to help you decide what you need. They should be able to discuss your business and your goals to help you identify the key aspects to put in a brief.

Be clear at the beginning what's included in their package, so you don't have a nasty surprise after the site has launched but is missing something important. Make sure in the initial stage that what you agree with the website developer is really what you want.

Clarify how they'll communicate with you during the project and their preferred method of reporting back to you. What are the project milestones to be aware of? Take the time to find the right person.

Look on a recruitment site for job descriptions for web designers. This will give you an idea of what they should be able to do. Contact their previous clients to find out what their experience of working with them was like.

Q: Should I buy all the domain names for my business?

If you're rebranding or relaunching a service, you'll want to purchase a domain name to go with it. When you look on the website domain selling sites, they'll often ask you if you want to buy the various domain name extensions too. So, along with .com or .co.uk, they'll offer you .edu, .tv, .biz, .org and so on.

Buying these does give you a bit of brand protection, but you also have to be conscious of the future – are you wanting to be global or are you wanting to be hyperlocal? It seems sensible to buy the .com and .co.uk along with something relevant to your industry, such as .marketing.

But there's really very little value in having those additional domain names other than to protect your brand. You can end up buying lots of domain names, spending hundreds and ultimately wasting your money.

It used to be true that .com and co.uk extensions were more trustworthy, but that's no longer the case, and multiple extensions don't do anything to increase your SEO, unless you're actually creating websites to go with all those URLs.

Leading on from that, people can then get bogged down into trying to decide what should go *before* the dot. Should it be the business name, the owner's name or the product or service you offer? Remember that the website is there to serve your business goals!

Having keywords in a domain name *can* help, but the bigger picture is what's the brand and what is the message you're trying to get across? What's the look and the size of the business?

Don't worry too much about trying to keyword stuff a domain name unless there's a really good reason to do so.
And remember, whatever URL you choose, your customers won't really care. What they really care about and really want is the information inside your site.

Q: How long does it take to build a website?

There are lots of adverts online at the moment claiming AI can build you a website in minutes, but we think that's unlikely. We've tested out different AI tools ourselves and downloaded the apps, so we know what's out there.

Sure, AI might be able to produce *something*, but how good will the result actually be? Will it be fit for purpose? Almost certainly not. AI can help to give a starting point and help with solving problems, but it can't create a whole website.

So how long does it take? Our advice is, take as long as you can within the parameters of your business strategies and your sales and marketing goals, because there is a real pleasure in developing the website at the right pace.

There's a need to gather the copy, photography, video assets, the product pages, staff bios and so on. That certainly can't be done in minutes, by you or by AI. The preparation stage is vital because it's often when you come up with the best solutions.

But there *is* room for an AI-powered solution that gives examples or suggestions about the future layout. You've then got a shortlist of layouts for various pages, and you can find suitable templates and layouts on your website builder.

Use AI to get over any blocks you've got around where to start, and use it to come up with ideas and a structure.

But part of the secret to being proud of your website is owning it. And unless you've owned it yourself and really invested that time and energy into it, you'll never feel proud of it.

The website is the door to your business and it should set the tone and personality. It also needs the functionality to solve business processes, capture data in the best way and engage with site visitors.

These are things that could get missed if you have a site built with AI. It might produce something that looks ok, but does it really get across the right message or really engage? Don't be fooled by the claims!

Q: What are avatars and should businesses use them?

An avatar or persona helps you to really understand your audience. Importantly, creating avatars can help you understand language used by your customers and, by extension, make your website and content relevant.

Avatars will also challenge how clear you are on what customers want and the outcome they're looking for when visiting your website.

It's always a worthwhile exercise to understand and define the personas your business has in its target audience, so you can identify the top two or three targets and the words they use to describe what you do.

The avatar, in brief, is a composite of all the qualities that your ideal customer has, gathered into one fictional character.

In some ways, the perfect scenario would be your own customers building your future website, because they are more likely to match the language, structure, photography, colours and more!

But as that won't happen just yet, we've been using avatars instead.

Top tip: Make these as visually interesting as possible, perhaps by choosing a photo of a person who matches your avatar. Try not to use a picture of someone famous or someone you know, though!

Being 'WebProud': When Curiosity Meets Action

Do you have more questions about running a successful website?

Do you want to access even more practical advice about SEO, content creation and website user experience?

It just so happens we have more answers for you, a lot more!

As mentioned, 'You Ask, We Answer' is the first segment of our '90-Day Website Mastery Podcast' and our collection of Q&As keeps expanding!

For more inspiration and clarity about the world of website management, head over to our official website https://90daymarketingmastery.com/video-podcast/

And don't forget to send us your questions too! We love nothing better than offering busy entrepreneurs and team leaders valuable lessons in feeling proud of your website again!

Jonny and Pascal

BONUS CONTENT 2

WEBSITE STORIES

In this bonus section, we go for a deep-dive into an article, a podcast, a video or a book and discuss the key lessons that can help anyone in charge of a website.

Consummate students of our art, we go through a countless number of content pieces in all media formats. Curated from our '90-Day Website Mastery Podcast', this selection was compiled with you, the busy entrepreneur or team leader, firmly in mind.

Many Business Owners are Embarrassed by Their Websites

A recent article by tech journalist Duncan McRae reported that 47% of UK businesses are embarrassed by their website when they have to show it to key stakeholders or customers.

This is something we hear all the time – being asked for their web address makes people anxious.

Furthermore, 92% believe their website's poor user experience is actually costing them money, and the vast majority are spending 3.5 hours a week fixing problems and errors on their websites.

This leads to a situation where people don't feel good about their website and aren't spending enough time on creating content. Constantly correcting errors is not a positive experience and creates a disconnect with the purpose of your site.

What's interesting about it is that somehow, we can get comfortable with being uncomfortable.

We're embarrassed by the website but we don't do much about it, because there's a lack of motivation and lack of understanding. Business owners have often had poor experiences with support, which puts them off asking for help.

There's an obvious lack of activity and commitment because unless they're blogging, people have no involvement with their website. They have it built and hosted and then forget about it for the most part.

Unless you're regularly updating a site so it's relevant to where your business is now, you *will* be embarrassed by it!

Access the original article here:
https://www.marketingtechnews.net/news/2023/jan/30/47-of-uk-businesses-are-embarrassed-by-their-website/

Three Traditional Marketing Tactics Making a Comeback

This is the title of an article by Emily Noel of studioID, and she celebrates this return, arguing that they have improved and evolved since they were first used in the 1990s.

The tactics are:
1. Direct mail
2. Cold email
3. The blog

We're so used to getting junk through our letterbox but there's a huge opportunity for direct mail right now. If you have a really targeted campaign, even if it's just 20 people, you could do well. We've seen campaigns like that with an 80% conversion rate.

You could argue that cold email is also very saturated, but if you can be very clear on your target audience and very precise in your message, cold email could absolutely be the answer for your business.

And with regard to blog writing, if you've got a piece of very resourceful content that's ultra helpful and shows you thoroughly understand your audience, blogs could do really well indeed.

If you want to build relationships, credibility and authority in the marketplace, you can't do that with just a few words. You have to be seen and heard to be helpful by going deep into a subject matter. So, let's focus on the blog part of the article.

Emily gives lots of examples, but she also says we can't just blog like we did in the 90s and 00s. We need to take it further, and we should also move away from calling it a 'blog', because there's so much more to it.

A better term, she says, is a 'content hub'.

The key point here is that no one prospect is the same, because different people consume content differently. So, you have to think about written, audio and video content, and present it in an organised way to make it easy for the visitor, which ties in with website design.

The future of blogging is more to do with being the administrator and architect of a home with a diverse range of content types that you've organised around themes and formats, which makes it easy for visitors to find what you do.

Access the original article here:
https://www.studioid.com/springboard/trends/3-traditional-marketing-tactics-making-a-comeback-2/

Five Secrets to Improve Your Website This Year

In a short and inspiring video, brand strategist and online communications expert Phil Pallen recommends five changes you should focus on right now.

1. **Be clearer:** On the homepage, above the fold, answer the questions: "Who are you? And why should I care?" in just two sentences. Capture the essence, the benefits of dealing with you before people have described for themselves.

2. **Accessibility is no longer an option**: There are lots of plugins available now that can help you remove any barriers to accessing the information on your website, such as accessiBe, which Phil recommends.

3. **Have better visuals:** To build trust and credibility and to attract the right customers, you need better, more beautiful photography.

4. **Make your call-to-action pages really stand out:** Phil means make it simple, clear and impactful. Spend time choosing the right images, design and layout.

5. **Follow accepted website best practice**: All the elements on a website you see all the time – layout, navigation, naming conventions, image positioning and so on – have come about because of studies on what the audience wants. Look at existing websites and notice what the experts have done.

This is about going back to basics and creating a website that Google will like and rank higher. Remember that you've got milliseconds to grab someone's attention, so these 'secrets' will help you do that.

The point Phil is making is that if you make an effort to do your research, to brief a photographer on what you want and really think about your website, that's a reflection of your own care in running the business and looking after customers.

People will make the link between the way it feels to visit a website and the future experience of dealing with you directly.

Access to the original video by Phil Pallen:
https://www.youtube.com/watch?v=FzbWWkuo2x8

Creating Helpful or Reliable People-First Content

This article was written by the team at Google Search Central, and it provides a list of questions you should ask yourself to make sure your content is really there to engage human beings rather than the search engines and the bots.

Historically, we've all been creating content that pleases the search spiders, and today we are being warned and advised that we should please people first.

With the rise of AI, where bots write the content for you, it's even more important right now to understand what Google is looking for in terms of good quality content.

The article provides an extensive list of questions to help you evaluate content that, ideally, is helpful, reliable, and people-first. Use their suggestions to assess your content and look at the quality, expertise you demonstrate and whether it's written people-first.

The article also recommends you get to know EEAT guidelines. This means you should create content that demonstrates:

- Evidence of experience
- Evidence of expertise
- Evidence of authority
- Evidence of trustworthiness

Finally, do you have content that explains the who, the how and the why? It's common sense, but it's well worth thinking about and discussing with your team.

As you review your content, consider if it provides original information reporting, research or analysis. If you've used external sources, have you avoided simply copying and rewriting those sources, and instead provided substantial additional value and originality? Does the main heading of the page provide a descriptive, helpful summary?

One of the main questions they want you to consider is: Who created the content? Is it self-evident to your visitors and does the page carry a byline where one might be expected? And do the bylines lead to further information on the author, giving background about them and the areas they write about?

This is all about providing evidence of expertise, trustworthiness and authority. Google wants you to make it abundantly clear who's written it, tell us a bit about them and why they're in a position to be able to give opinion on whatever they write about. Then, let visitors find out more about the author and get to know them.

Remember too that there's nothing wrong with using AI content; it's about *how* you use it and what you do with it. By all means use it to give you the framework of a blog, but mention on the page that you did so, and add something that indicates you as the author edited and fact-checked it.

Access the original article here:
https://developers.google.com/search/docs/fundamentals/creating-helpful-content

Google I/O Annual Conference

Google I/O is a full day conference where the department heads at Google reveal what they've got coming up across all the Google products we use daily.

It can be very technical, but there's often some good insight into what is about to change with website indexing, Google Maps and other marketing channels.

For marketers and web editors, it's great to be forewarned and make adjustments accordingly.

In case you didn't know, Google's mission is to organise the world's information to make it universally accessible and useful. At one of the recent conferences, the VP of Engineering, Cathy Edwards, gave an update on generative AI.

Very soon, when you search for something on Google, along with the usual buttons for 'news', 'images', 'shopping' and so on, there'll be a button labelled 'converse', and that means you can have a conversation with Bard, the behind-the scenes AI machinery.

You can speak directly to it so search can be done by voice, and it can be long-tail questions. Bard (now Google Gemini) will respond to you, and you can ask follow-up questions. Bard can also give you suggestions on what your follow-up questions should be, and it will pull up results from across the internet.

It means you can give Google a lot of information upfront to give you really specific results. For instance, rather than just asking for a restaurant in a particular location, you can ask it to find one that's also dog-friendly, suitable for families, in a certain price range and so on. You don't have to find that extra detail yourself.

As Cathy herself said: "This is search super-charged, but for the user."

This is going to become the norm quite soon, and it is a complete game changer. The prospect of no longer being listed on the search results pages is certainly very daunting for all of us.

It remains that Google can only reply to questions with information it has gathered from your website and associated platforms. So, as a business owner, you need to take the initiative and publish relevant answers to questions so Google can find you and present you to the searcher. If you do not, you're moving backwards in your website mastery journey, not forwards.

Access the original keynote presentation here:
Google I/O Annual Conference – Spotlight on Search + AI
https://www.youtube.com/live/cNfINi5CNbY?feature=share&t=2436

Strategies for Bloggers

This article, originally entitled *New Blogging Statistics: What Content Strategies Work? We asked 1016 Bloggers,* comes from Orbit Media, one of our all time go-to authorities when it comes to website experience.

Every year, they do a huge piece of research where they interview over 1,000 bloggers about their tactics and strategies. Here are just three to get you started.

1. **The ideal length for a blog:** The more words you have and the more you can expand on a point, the better the results. Anything between 1,500 and 3,000 words is what to aim for.

2. **The content types for the best results:** How-to articles, lists, guides and eBooks come out top, closely followed by news and trends, and interviews.

3. **The ideal number of visuals:** The longer your post, the more images you need. At least six images is good, but more is also fine.

This also helps to encourage people to stay on a page for longer and engage with your content, and shows Google that people like spending time on your site.

You could even go back to some of your older, well-performing content and look at making them longer using the techniques mentioned.

However, here are some words of caution (pun intended!).

Firstly, don't just add words for the sake of it. A long blog post should give real value to the reader.

And secondly, do not neglect completely shorter form content. Some of the best blogs only have a couple of hundred words; for instance, a piece of news or a particular story can be better suited to a shorter post.

Top tip: research and seek out the latest reports on blogging statistics from Orbit Media; it is really worth it.

Access the original article here:
https://www.orbitmedia.com/blog/blogging-statistics/

Four Reasons No One is Reading Your Content

This is the title of an article published on PR Daily by Alison Carter. Here are her reasons:

1. Your headline or subject line is boring
2. You published at the wrong time
3. Your story is in the wrong format
4. The story is not relevant to your audience

1. Your headline: Where do people go wrong with the headline? There are two main mistakes we see people make. The first is that you've been too generous and the headline gives everything away, so there is no motivation for the audience to read on.

Or you've gone the other way, and you're so secretive that there's nothing in there for the audience to get excited about and it comes across as a bit dull. The solution is to reread your story and go back and change your headline.

2. The time: What is the wrong time to publish a blog? There's all sorts of research that explains the best day of the week and time of day, but these are global studies with a large dataset. You can't be sure that your audience will behave in the same way.

Instead, use your analytics data to help you find out when people check their emails, look at social media or visit a website. You can then marry up your publishing schedule accordingly and learn by testing. Also, the time of day you publish a post on your website is less important than the time you share it on social media to get the most views of it.

3. Story in wrong format: In a perfect world, every story we share would be created in different formats for different audiences. But that's not achievable for many of us. Time is a resource we don't have enough of. This is where a good content promotion and repurposing strategy comes in handy.

You also need to learn from the audience. If your content is too long, think about making it shorter or use video. If they don't watch video, think about writing. People will have a preferred format.

4. You're irrelevant: Remember that ultimately a website project is not a technical project, it's a human interaction project. The more you want to learn about the audience, the more content you produce, and sometimes it'll be a dud. When that happens, learn from it and ask yourself:

- Why didn't it work on this occasion?
- What prompted me to do this content?
- Was I under pressure from the client or boss?
- Was I following a trend that I misread?
- Did I rush it?
- How can I communicate better the next time around?
- Did I create it just for the sake of it?
- Did I have a purpose for the content?

Access the original article here: https://www.prdaily.com/4-reasons-no-one-is-reading-your-content/

22 Types of Content You Should Create to Reach Your Audience

This is an infographic from Giraffe Social Media, reviewed by Social Media Today's Mark Walker-Ford. The title infers that this is content for social media, but we want content that you'll share on your website as curation.

The Giraffe Team have split the content type into stages in the customer journey:

1. Awareness stage
2. Consideration stage
3. Decision stage
4. Retention stage

Don't forget that, depending on the mindset and where they are in their decision-making process, you have different ways to engage your audience.

For instance, in the awareness stage this could be about exploring the what and why of a problem that needs a solution as well as discovering your existence for the first time.

During the consideration stage, you can use different content types such as authored blog posts, infographics, podcasts, eBooks, checklists and white papers. These are all used to help your prospects match your organisation against the visitor's needs.

Content pieces like case studies, demo videos and quizzes, product webinars and white papers come into the decision stage, where they choose you as part of the perfect solution. There are also tactics like free trials, live demos, consultations, coupons for trial before you buy, testimonials, and comparison sheets.

The retention stage is after-sales care to change the occasional buyer into a regular customer or champion of your business. This stage would include ongoing support, online chats, coupons, loyalty rewards and email follow up.

It's so important to understand the funnel and where people are on the buyer journey.

You need to guide them through that so they can start to know, like and trust you – so content specific to each stage is essential.

Top tip: Once someone becomes a customer, take the time to show them ways to get more value from what they've purchased. You might want to give them access to a VIP section of the website they can log into for more helpful content.

Access the original infographic here:
https://www.socialmediatoday.com/news/22-content-create-reach-audience-infographic/652639/

The Future of SEO With AI-Powered Search

It seems fitting that we should end this bonus section with a LinkedIn video by entrepreneur Rand Fishkin. In it, Rand explains how businesses can be effective with SEO even when their audience is using AI-powered search tools.

"The keyword here is *co-occurrence*, making sure that your brand shows up in and around the words and phrases that large language models get trained on. They produce word tokens which are likely to appear after, and sometimes, other word tokens.

"If you go to Bing and search for 'the best hotel deals', you'll get results of real places, but it'll also show you *websites* that offer good deals, such as Kayak, Trivago and Expedia.

"If you then go to Google, it will show you a very similar subset, because these are the brands that have built language co-occurrence. They're the words, part of sentences and characters that are likely to show up.

"But if you ask ChatGPT the same question, it'll give you a list of text that is most likely to appear near other words and extracts around the same subject.

"But this isn't knowledge and these aren't answers, it's the same data as Bing and Google."

Rand's video is a reminder that this is all about context. If you're talking about a particular topic or subject, you want to ensure you know the top 10 pages that rank for your topic. Look at what else they talk about, and make sure you are also seen and heard being helpful about those topics too.

For example, an estate agent might find that the top 10 pages about estate agents also talk about mortgages and insurance. So, you need to make sure that if you're creating an estate agent page, you're also discussing and explaining mortgages and insurance.
Doing so helps the AI understand that you are relevant, because you're talking about all these other topics that are related to the content.

If you want to rank well for a particular subject, you've got to rank well for the things around that subject too.

If you have a brand name, what is the qualifying strapline that normally goes alongside that? If you have several products, make sure your name is associated with all of them and that none of the products are being neglected. You want to have the right words connected to your name.

As Rand says: "So long term, marketers are going to associate their brand with topics and content and concepts all across the web, so that the large language models pick them up in order for search results to include them."

Access the original video here:
https://www.linkedin.com/posts/randfishkin_if-i-had-to-guess-what-marketers-will-be-activity-7086801513712345088-CbDA

Dive Deeper into Website Mastery

If you found this bonus section insightful and thought-provoking and would welcome accessing a few more, you're in luck!

Our '90-Day Website Mastery Podcast' continues to expand its collection of content reviews and deep-dives, and we are glad to be able to offer more inspiration and clarity about the world of website design and management.

To access even more expert views, reactions and actionable insights, visit our official website at https://90daymarketingmastery.com/video-podcast/.

Don't miss this opportunity to enhance your website skills and stay ahead of changes in the digital world. And remember, we welcome your suggestions – your curiosity drives our content!

Jonny and Pascal

BONUS CONTENT 3

WEBSITE ENGINE ROOM

You can't be as passionate about website design and management as we are, and not be interested in the latest app or tech tool that can make your life easier as the website manager and content creator.

In this section, inspired by the 'Website Mastery' podcast conversations, we share a curated list of 20 online solutions that will make a huge difference to your productivity and the performance of your website.

Read to the end for a free gift!

SEMrush

A platform that enables you to get measurable results from online marketing. Giving you the ability to do SEO, content marketing, competitor research, PPC and social media marketing.

The data available is so useful because it helps with competitor analysis, keywords and any gaps, ranking, content suggestions and monitoring error handling. More importantly, it tracks who's linking to your website and what they are saying about you. It will also flag any links you don't want to have.

SEMrush can look at your content and identify where you're missing a paragraph in a blog about a particular topic, or areas on your website that need keywords. It can even highlight where you should be linking to your own content elsewhere on your site.

It's also a nice reminder that your website is an extension of your approach to customer service. If you know for a fact that people have questions that haven't been answered or could be answered more fully, this tool can help you do that.

Top Tip: It's important to note that SEMrush is an expensive tool, so it's an investment you might not want to make at the moment. However, there is a free trial that lets you get the data you need. You could pay for a month, or find someone else with a subscription to let you use theirs.

CapCut

CapCut is an all-in-one video editing mobile app, but they've also released a desktop version, which is really good.

CapCut has lots of templates, transitions and easy to use editing features you can use to create visual stories that can supplement your blog section, your 'About' and 'Meet the Team' pages.

Video is a very important content format to build trust and credibility; it ranks well but it has multiple uses. It shows you've taken the time to create a good visual story, which the audience will really appreciate. CapCut is great if you're new to video editing, but there are some really good advanced features too.

Top Tip: One of the reasons CapCut is helpful for content creators is because everyone has a ton of photos and videos on their mobile phones, often taken for use on social media, and you can now convert all that media into animated visual stories!

Lapa.Ninja

We all need a nudge in the right direction when it comes to finding inspiration and move away from the competition! Lapa.Ninja is run by a bunch of enthusiastic individuals who go around the Internet taking screenshots of landing pages they like.

They have more than 5,000 examples of great landing pages to inspire you!

We always recommend looking at other industries, because you might see something completely different that you will be drawn to. When that happens, think about why you're drawn to it, and see if you can bring those lessons into your own website experience.

Top Tip: Remember that you don't have to reinvent the wheel. It's about taking some of the best and creating something even better using your imagination.

Canva

The design tool Canva isn't new, but so many people still aren't using it fully or have not even heard of it. We'd recommend investing in the pro version, which is around £100, because there are so many templates, images, graphics and resources available.

And it's not just images for graphic design! You can create videos, social media posts, PowerPoint presentations and record videos. It makes content creation so much quicker and easier if you're managing a website.

Top Tip: Even if you are a regular user of Canva, you probably have the same templates that you go to every time. Canva, like many platforms, keeps releasing new features and templates so often that they're easy to miss.

Postmark CX

One of the things a lot of people don't consider are the emails their website sends. For example, if you fill out a form, or if you purchase a product, it then sends automated emails to say: "Thanks for filling this form out, someone will be in contact." Or perhaps it says: "Thanks for your order. Here's your order history." Those are what we call transactional emails.

In a lot of cases, the transactional emails are just sent from the website on the website server. This leads to two things:

1. Poor deliverability: the chance of your user receiving these transactional emails can be really low.

2. You're not helping Google: it will regard some of these emails as spam, because it's coming from the web server's IP address. If that happens, the IP can be black-listed, which has an impact on your ranking.

To protect your website's trustworthiness, authority and respect, take those transactional emails out of the equation completely. We recommend an app called Postmark CX from Active Campaign, which costs around $10 a month. It ensures the deliverability of your email and protects your reputation.

Answer the Public

A lot of people are using AI tools to write their content for them, and there are both positives and negatives to this, but it does have a bearing on people's ability to check you out in the verification phase of making a buying decision.

Say they've been on your website and checked you out and they're just about ready to buy, but they're not quite there. So the AI tool helps them to find out more about you. They don't have to spend ages on Google trying to find the right phrase to help them with their search.

Instead, they can paraphrase what they're looking for and ask AI to present a summary of your business – your people, its overall performance, if there have been any complaints, reviews and so on.

But this means there's pressure on website managers to create more content that is also timely and meaningful, which, ultimately, means coming up with more content ideas, which can be time-consuming.

Fortunately, the website Answer The Public can help.

Answer the Public is effectively a social listening tool that tracks what people search for on Google and other hubs, monitoring the keywords and phrases they use and presenting the information in a mindmap layout.

Top Tip: Explore the different segments and sectors and note down your ideas. You could use it alongside an AI tool but you need to do the writing yourself, otherwise there's a risk of plagiarism and unoriginal content.

Tawk.to

This is a free-to-use live chatbot that's simple to use and, when used correctly, can really add value to your website.

Remember that nowadays visitors use websites in a different way. They want quick answers and interaction, so live chat allows you to start engaging very quickly with a potential customer. Explore the Tawk.to tool and see what it can do.

Top Tip: People sometimes get live chat wrong by pretending a visitor is talking to a team member rather than a bot. Be honest and let people know that at certain times you're unavailable and the chatbot will take over.

Visme.co

This is a platform dedicated to converting complex messages and sometimes data into engaging visual stories, and the templates are really impressive. But we have a very different suggestion for you.

Before you record a video, it's always a good idea to storyboard what you're going to do. Visme.co can be used for a number of visual types of content. They've recently launched a free storyboard creator, so you can create some static visuals to illustrate the point you want to make via a moving image.

Top Tip: Visme.co would also be helpful if you decide to revamp your 'About Us' page, as you can use it with the team and plan out your next storytelling content. It might also point out where you need to work a bit harder on some of the key messages.

Google Search Console

This isn't a new tool, but it's something we think is essential for anyone serious about having an effective website. You can't speak to Google directly about search engine optimisation

(SEO), but the Console *does* open a door to structured two-way communication.

It allows Google to tell you what they know about your site and what they think of it. Basically, they point out any errors you need to fix. You can also tell Google if you want to have a page removed from the index or look for security issues.

It's also an information and data-rich tool, as it gives a lot of valuable information:

- How often you're shown in search results
- Which keywords you're shown for
- The click-through rate

Top Tip: Open a Google Search Console account and break down the different areas of the summary dashboard, starting with the urgent website fixes and then moving onto content of interest to your audience. Organise an action plan with specific dates and continuously monitor the positive impact of your changes.

re:Bloom

A lot of our clients want to refresh their websites. Sometimes they have new products and services to add; other times they think it looks outdated. But it's not always easy to know where to begin.

A tool called re:Bloom can help. It's designed for people who have built their websites on Web Flow with support by Figma, but the advice will work on any system.

re:Bloom has created a template library, where they have broken down the website into its component parts – homepage, contact us, landing, pricing, about us pages – and they give you elegant wireframes that you can use for inspiration.

Top Tip: You can use them how you like – organise, print, save and screenshot. And, rather than just having a vague idea that the 'About' page needs a better layout, you have something you can use to start a conversation with people.

Zoho CRM

Many businesses have a CRM but they're not using it as well as they should and it hasn't been properly integrated. This means their data is not easily accessible and not as helpful as it could be.

You need a customer relationship manager tool that is going to really help you understand your customers, clients, potential customers, leads and so on. A tool like Zoho lets you see where a lead came from, the conversion, how to keep them engaged and more.

Plus, there are add-ons for automated email campaigns, sales, accounts and marketing. Whether you choose Zoho or another CRM, think about how you can connect your website to a CRM so the whole thing is seamless.

When someone fills out a form, makes a phone call or sends an email, the whole journey is fully understood, so you can market to them at every single touch point, and start segmenting from day one.

A good CRM can also help you to successfully onboard a new employee, with part of the induction dedicated to getting them up to speed with the existing customer base, prospects and so on.

Top Tip: Don't scrimp on the CRM you choose. There are different packages at different price points, and at the beginning you might not think you need it all. But it's better to think about integrating as much as possible right from the get-go.

Trello

Trello is an incredible information and project management board, where you can organise the stages of a project and the flow in a very visual way. It's a lot more inspiring than a list in a Google Doc or an Excel spreadsheet.

You can add photos, hyperlinks and videos. You can reorganise the cards in any way you like, assign tasks and share it all with your team. It's a much more stimulating tool than the traditional ones, and great for collaboration.

Top Tip: Reflect and research all the different new ideas and project plans being recorded and stored, then challenge yourself and investigate whether a visual dashboard would be more helpful.

Google Books

A big task for website editors is to curate content and add citations from published authors. This helps with credibility and adds interest to the article, podcast or video.

There is a little known service called Google Books, which is like a mini search engine specialising in published work. It allows you to scan books using keywords or a short phrase and bring up passages, paragraphs and citations from books.

If you're explaining how to do something, or if you want to comment on a news item and you want to illustrate your point by quoting work by an expert, Google Books will find you interesting sources.

Top Tip: Make sure you capture and share the title and author, the publication date and so on, making your citation in line with copyright and good journalism. You can then copy and paste whatever you need and feature it at the bottom of your article.

What People Ask.net

This is a free and alternative version of Answer the Public, the tool that lets you find out what people are searching for. It's a great way to be able to get information from a large dataset without spending hours on the Internet.

Top Tip: Remember that when people search on Google, they're looking for a solution to their problems, or an answer to their practical questions. Knowing what they are looking for means you can plan a weekly or monthly content series around that subject for even greater engagement.

Scribe

Many business owners will delegate their website management and content creation to colleagues or an external supplier. But how do you explain how you do what you do? You might have a Zoom call, record a video walk-through of the CRM, create a step-by-step guide. All of this is very time-consuming.
Now, imagine if you had an assistant sitting next to you writing down what you'd say to someone in need of a step-by-step guide. What Scribe does is a screen capture as you go through the process of completing an activity, and it also puts annotations over each step, which you can edit once you've finished.

It gives you the best of two worlds: a visual guide, but with static images (because video can be tricky to follow in a tutorial) and a written guide with the annotations.

There's a free Chrome extension, but you might find the features in the paid-for version meet your business needs.

Top Tip: As well as using it internally with staff, you could use it externally to help customers who are struggling to log in to a website or find their way around a new platform, or nervous about using a payment system they are not familiar with.

SEOquake

SEO is a huge opportunity for businesses, and it's not just about written content.

SEOquake.com has an extension you can add to Firefox or

Chrome and while you're googling for information, it adds another layer of data onto your Google screen against every single website that appears on the search results giving you all the key metrics on the page. Pretty clever stuff!

Top Tip: Don't spend your time just looking at competitors' websites; explore the data from websites your visitors are likely to visit, from news to advice and complementary services.

Post Genius

Post Genius is an AI-powered solution that helps stimulate your imagination by suggesting alternative versions to your social media posts, which is great when you work on your own or are up against a deadline!

We have a great idea for you: Post Genius can help you get more testimonials and case studies for your website.

Simply write the first version of what a recent client would say about their experience, then copy and paste it into Post Genius to get some different versions. You can then add these into an email to your client and ask them to choose their preferred version, making the process quicker.

Link Whisper

Linkwhisper.com is an internal linking tool to speed up the process of internal linking for search engine optimisation and, ultimately, to help you rank better. There's a WordPress plugin and it works on Shopify.

It integrates with Yoast and Rank Math, which are the two leading SEO plugins, and it just makes it abundantly easy to create internal links. If you're writing a blog post or a new service page, as you're writing it identifies link opportunities to other parts of your website.

Internal linking is often forgotten about on websites because the focus is on the look, the feel, how it works and the words, but it's where the biggest opportunity is to shape Google's thoughts about what pages should rank and the importance of those pages.

Top Tip: Review your website content and main sections and identify pages, in particular in your blog and products/services, that should be linking with each other as they share similar themes and complement each other.

HubSpot Templates for Creating Avatars

Customer avatars, or personas, can be enigmatic terms, but this stage of your website design or refresh project is crucial.

By understanding and paraphrasing your target audience's needs, goals and pain points, you can genuinely tailor your website content, navigation and overall design to be more user-friendly and engaging.

The online marketing platform HubSpot has taken the trouble to put together some great templates for PowerPoint and Microsoft Word that give blank boxes to fill in.

It's a good way to get started with your buyer personas. We would also recommend reviewing your avatars before you make any major changes to your website.

Top Tip: Focus on quality over quantity. Develop a few detailed customer personas that accurately represent your ideal customers rather than a large number of generic ones. Trust us, we've made that mistake in the past.

'WebProud': Mastering the Right Tech for your Website Experience

We hope this curated list of 20 online solutions, inspired by our '90-Day Website Mastery Podcast' conversations, helps boost your productivity and website performance.

But why stop here?

To dive deeper into the world of website solutions and to hear about our latest suggestions, visit our official podcast for more expert tech reviews and advice: https://90daymarketingmastery.com/video-podcast/

And don't miss out on our free 'Ultimate Website Toolkit' ebook, with 50 website tech and apps that will make your life easier and help you feel proud of your website again: https://90daymarketingmastery.com/e-book/

Download it now to explore a treasure trove of tech solutions designed to streamline your tasks and accelerate content creation.

Your journey to being 'WebProud' would not be complete without the right tech!

Jonny and Pascal

BONUS CONTENT 4

WEBSITE CALL TO ACTION

Inspired by countless conversations with coaching clients, we would like to present to you a year-long website experience roadmap!

One simple change, one simple action for you to undertake each week.

You will be able to select from the list below a practical activity to elevate your website, from reviewing recent achievements to creating interactive infographics, and these changes will deliver a significant impact, making your website work harder and yield better results.

Are you ready for a digital makeover that will reshape how you perceive and experience your online presence? Ready to feel proud of your website again?

Let's begin...

1. Review your achievements for the past six months and make sure your website is updated accordingly, from new client logos to sales copy and team biographies.

2. Create a storyboard of your website experience, a highlight of the content sections, the functionality, and value-added elements that make it so unique – then compile a video tour using Canva!

3. Go back to your content and identify which pages performed well at the same time last year, then relaunch the pages with additional media content, clearer paragraphs, better optimisation, quotes, stats, etc. That's what we call 'repurposing up'!

4. Review and create three types of profiles for everyone in your organisation: 1) bylines, 2) guest summaries, and 3) full biographies. Ideal for social posts or team pages.

5. Research the key historical events and inventions in your industry and add nostalgia to your content marketing activities. This is very powerful and always gets great reactions!

6. Do a Google search and collate the options from the 'People Also Ask' and 'Related Searches' panels (and, soon, AI-powered suggestions such as 'Follow-Up Questions').

7. Organise the results from last week's research into groups and themes. Next step: research stats and trends associated with these questions to compile in-depth 'how to' articles series.

8. Look back at your best performing social media posts and consider two content 'repurposing up' tactics: 1) embed the posts in relevant website articles, and 2) create a brand new long-form blog inspired by the post and reactions.

9. Time for a mid-year review of your case studies and testimonials. Look back at completed projects over the past six months and compile a list of stories to produce over the coming weeks.

10. Work on your out-of-office messages for the year. Lean on your unique tone of voice and write a short article about what your customers should focus on during the summer or Christmas seasons.

11. Organise an in-person team meeting or join a virtual mastermind group to come up with your next core themes and hooks for your content marketing, from blog/vlog series to social media posts.

12. Check the origin of your inbound links and citations. Make a list and decide which online brands should be highlighted on your website, on a press release or in your pitch deck. Get in touch to suggest collaborating on more content.

13. Make a list of your memberships, trade associations, awards, certifications, etc. and check whether the

logos and spotlight articles explaining their values to your clients are present on your website.

14. Create a research project team (e.g. use local universities) and find your national and international data sources for industry retrospectives and forecasts – curate the stats for your next content push!

15. Launch a dedicated section on your website as a comprehensive resource hub for global trade, with guides, market insights and regulatory updates relevant to your industry and clients.

16. Get a report on your best-performing web pages and check whether the 'alt text' field for your visuals needs improving and rewriting. Talk to your website designer about introducing Schema markups.

17. Look back at your mission statement and brand values. Are they featured sufficiently on your website? Do you need to create a manifesto page to highlight your 'why'?

18. Organise a meeting with your customer-facing teammates and list all the questions they frequently answer. This will provide you with the structure for your next free eBook.

19. Study your website dashboard and spot the best-performing articles with the title 'how to...' or similar. Next step: add a free download/template and reshare the article.

20. Research how to design and publish interactive infographics to present all your data and numerical information in a more dynamic way. Your visitors will thank you for it!

21. Review and rethink the layout and style of your website footer, and make sure to include the year your business started and the current year in your copyright statement.

22. First, compile a draft article looking back and looking ahead at the next 12 months. Next, send the draft to your customers and influencers for their reactions. Then publish the finished article with their comments and reactions. Finally, share on social media with all contributors and sources tagged.

23. Research blog header images from other sectors and industries. See anything you like? Go ahead and use them as inspiration to modernise the design and look of your own blog series.

24. Do you embed videos from YouTube on your website? Do you hate the suggested videos feature at the end? Reduce distractions by adding ?rel=0 to your video web address.

25. Check that Google Analytics 4 conversion tracking has been set up properly. Use the additional visitor insights to adjust your webpages in order to increase engagement and conversion rates.

26. Time for another review to create new case studies and testimonials. Look back at completed projects

over the past six months and compile a list of contacts and stories to produce in the next quarter.

27. Boost your WordPress website's speed and performance today by integrating NitroPack.io. The faster load times and optimised site efficiency will really improve user experience and search rankings.

28. Boost your local and therefore overall presence in Google by creating locally targeted content, such as a list of local events, industry bodies and news roundups.

29. Revisit and refresh your call-to-action buttons – it's time to ensure they're as engaging and effective as possible. A small tweak can lead to a big leap in user interaction and more requests for information.

30. Are you making full use of Google Search Console and the additional data it provides? It's not perfect but it will encourage you to reflect on simple things you could do to improve your visibility.

31. Review your hosting SLAs and performance. If need be, upgrade your hosting package – you want fast, reliable, trustworthy hosting that works for all territories.

32. Double-check the font size of your H1s. Make sure they are the biggest element on your webpage and display relevant and engaging copy.

33. Take a moment to update your website's homepage. When was the last time you updated the above the fold section, the photography, the layout, the copy?

34. Review and update your website's legal pages, including data protection compliance, privacy policy, terms and conditions and cookie policy. Keeping these crucial elements current promotes legal integrity and user trust.

35. Conduct a thorough check for broken links on your website. Fixing them makes a difference to how visitors will feel about your website, boosts SEO, and maintains the professionalism of your online presence.

36. Test your website's forms and email automations. Make sure they work seamlessly, not only to improve user experience but also to safeguard the effectiveness of your lead generation and customer communication.

37. Take a moment to load your website on different mobile devices and double-check its functionality. We know that mobile responsiveness and ease of use is key to engaging the growing number of mobile users effectively.

38. Improve your website's readability by breaking up content with bullet points and subheadings. This simple change can significantly increase user engagement and content absorption.

39. Ask a native speaker to go through your translated and localised website content, in particular the

optimised copy with keywords targeting your global audience.

40. Refresh your website's appeal by updating your photography style. New, high-quality images can rejuvenate your site's look, reflect recent changes, and re-engage your existing audience with a fresh visual perspective.

41. When was the last time you checked and challenged the design of your 'Contact Us' page? Research and bookmark examples from other sectors and use them as inspiration for your own website.

42. Add more relevant internal links between web pages. This not only helps Google understand the importance of your pages but also makes it so much easier for your visitors to access more content they are interested in.

43. Do you have a current website favicon that clearly represents your brand? This small but vital element really helps with brand recognition and professionalism in browser tabs and bookmarks.

44. Add an autocomplete advanced filter search to assist your website visitors. This upgrade makes navigating your content more intuitive and efficient for all users.

45. Revitalise your website's design by adding more empty space. This not only reduces clutter but also enhances readability and gives your content room to breathe, creating a more user-friendly experience.

46. If you have checkouts or forms with multiple steps on your website, add progress indicators to provide clear updates and guidance. This will reassure visitors and increase the completion rates.

47. Find out about your best-performing publicly available free downloads and offer this valuable content behind a signup form to generate leads. It feels counter-intuitive but it does work!

48. Boost your website's visual appeal by adding very subtle animations and transitions. These can bring your pages to life, guide users' attention and improve the overall interactive experience.

49. Simplify how visitors can access your site navigation when scrolling through your pages by implementing a 'sticky menu' that remains visible at the top of all pages.

50. Create a content roundup article – in other words, a collection of related articles or products summarised with links to the full version. These themed roundups are so helpful to visitors and create a truly engaging browsing experience.

51. Increase your website content visibility by implementing Schema Markups, talk to your website designers or do your research to find out about ways to improve onsite SEO and appeal with rich snippets in search results.

52. Take a positive step towards accessibility: shortlist your best performing articles, use AI to create written summaries and convert them into audio or video versions. Then embed the audio and video files below your article header graphics.

EXTRA: Consider implementing helpful exit pop-ups on your website. These can be a strategic tool to capture attention or offer value as visitors are about to leave, potentially increasing engagement and conversions.

There you have it, and well done for going through this entire list. Which actions will you do first, and what did you find most inspiring? Do you have your own suggestions? Send us your ideas for future publications.

Remember, your website is an extension of your customer service experience and a testament to how much you care about your online audience and their experience online and in-person.

Being WebProud: Completing One Action at a Time

We hope you are as excited as we are about using this year-long website experience roadmap. We truly believe it offers you a powerful path to feeling proud of your website again.

With 52 simple yet impactful actions, you have everything you need to create a greater connection between your audience and your website, week by week.

But what if you want more? What if you have already completed most of the actions?

We've got an exciting solution for you called 'Action Randomizer'.

Visit our official website at https://90daymarketingmastery.com/roll-the-dice/ and try it out now. It's so simple and so powerful!

With just a click, you'll 'roll the dice' to discover the ONE change you should make to your website right now.

You'll be presented with a corresponding video where we personally describe the activity we recommend, ensuring you learn something new and make a meaningful improvement today.

Don't let another day pass without improving your digital presence – and new website calls to action are added all the time – so roll the dice now and never run out of ideas for your website's transformation project!

Jonny and Pascal

CONGRATULATIONS

You've conquered all four chapters of the "For Imagination" section of the 'WebProud' practical guide!

Thank you for taking the time to explore practical website management answers, reflect on thought-provoking content dives, unearth over 20 difference-making tools and tech solutions, and discover 50 website tweaks to make you beam with pride.

Imagine the possibilities when you put this newfound knowledge into action! Imagine what it feels like to become 'WebProud'!

Want more ideas and inspiration for your website?

1. Try our Interactive 'Action Randomizer' Tool

Roll the dice to discover one actionable tip and watch a corresponding video to implement it today.
https://90daymarketingmastery.com/roll-the-dice/

2. Download the ULTIMATE Website Toolkit E-Book

Discover 50 handpicked tools to help you feel proud of your website again. This e-book provides tech and apps designed to simplify tasks, improve performance, and speed up content creation. https://90daymarketingmastery.com/e-book/

3. **Ready to Supercharge Your Website Even Further?**

Head over to our website: https://90daymarketingmastery.com/

Transform your digital marketing in just 90 days! This programme is ideal for marketing and sales professionals in various industries.

- **Boost Sales:** Optimise your website for better lead generation.
- **Gain Confidence:** Master the latest digital marketing strategies.
- **Clarity and Action:** Learn where to start and how to measure success. Includes expert-led training, practical tools, and access to exclusive podcasts and e-books.

We Want to Hear From You!

Got questions or a success story to share? **Connect with us on social media and let's celebrate how these website strategies have transformed your digital space into a website you can be truly proud of!**

Simply search for 'Jonny Ross' or 'Pascal Fintoni' – we can easily be found online.

Jonny and Pascal

FINAL THOUGHTS

As mentioned at the very beginning of this practical guide, on 30th April 1993 the Internet was born – or, more precisely, the World Wide Web project was made public by English computer scientist Tim Berners-Lee and his colleagues at CERN.

This most incredible invention inspired the original idea for this closing section, which was to look back at the contribution made by the many men and women who have helped shape the future of doing business over the past thirty years.

However, this significant milestone remained largely unnoticed as the news headlines in the world of technology were then, and still are, completely dominated by a global phenomenon with the shortest of acronyms: AI.

Artificial Intelligence, or, as we sometimes call it, Artificial Imitation, seems to continuously capture the interest and curiosity of so many. Understandably, opinions vary on the impact of AI on society and business, from apocalyptic predictions to idealistic visions, making it difficult to reach a position on the subject.

Having been involved in the adoption of new technologies for three decades, we have been able to track as best we can the evolution of machine learning and tested countless AI solutions. Personally, we think the truth is somewhere in the middle, although this time it does feel a little different.

The AI-Powered Online Experience

It is a fascinating subject, but we need to turn our attention to the impact of AI on our marketing and sales activities, in particular online. This is, after all, our specialist area and the environment where we are going to see the most significant change in behaviour – especially the ability for our customers and prospects to not only search but also verify information about our businesses to a degree and to an extent we have not witnessed so far.

Let's use an obvious example – Google – and let's consider their future plans.

We have all experienced first-hand the presence of machine learning and AI in the Google ecosystem, from the reasonably helpful auto-complete feature of Gmail to the very practical auto-suggest elements of the Google Search results and more. These instances, and many others, still rely on our willingness to put sufficient effort into typing, shortlisting, reviewing, gathering, doing secondary searches, etc.

In other words, we are limited by time and resources.

In early May 2023, the future Google AI-powered search experience was demonstrated during the annual Google I/O conference in Mountain View, California. It was a real eye opener to what will be possible soon by simply having a conversation, in the written form to begin with, but very quickly using voice and sign language.

Using the same amount of time and resources as we do currently with our 'mechanical' attempts, the depth and breadth of information about you and your activities that will be gathered and organised will be nothing short of staggering.

The AI-Powered Online Buyer

Yesterday, your prospects were typing your business name into a search engine.

Today, your prospects will simply say:

"Give me a summary of the activities of [enter your business] over the past three years. Can you list their financial information in a separate document for my credit control team, and can you list the main contacts working at [enter your business] and add their LinkedIn profile URLs and any recent social media posts and articles they have published on their website. Finally, in a PowerPoint presentation style, can you summarise for me which companies they are already supplying in [enter region] and who the main contacts are. I want to find out about their experience of dealing with [enter your business]."

If we were in a room together, we would probably pause right now. Not for effect, but to give you the time and space to process this new scenario, this new reality.

Observing your body language and listening to the faint murmur of conversations, we would most likely pick up two reactions or mindsets:

Reaction number 1: Brilliant! Let them check us out. We've been investing consistently in our online presence and e-reputation. I must let my colleagues know that all their hard work in content creation across our website, social media and other platforms is worthwhile and we must keep going.

Reaction number 2: Oops! I guess this might be the wake-up call and business case I have been looking for to launch or reset our online marketing efforts. I must talk to my colleagues about moving faster with our digital marketing plans, from our website experience to social media and outreach campaigns.

In both cases, the logical conclusion is that no matter which AI solution is favoured by your customers in the future, the search results depend entirely on the existence of multimedia information created by you and by others, published on platforms you control, including your website.

In truth, there will be a third reaction and realisation: how you might leverage the speed and usefulness of Artificial Intelligence to improve the efficacy of your existing technologies and, as a result, create a better website experience for your clients and colleagues alike.

The aim? Getting ready for *AI-Powered Website Visitors and Buyers.*

Although this closing remark is a complete departure from the original idea of celebrating the World Wide Web being made public by Sir Tim Berners-Lee, we think it is fitting nonetheless to leave the final words to him:

"When something is such a creative medium as the web, the limits to it are our imagination."

To your success.

Jonny Ross and Pascal Fintoni

Gratitude and Acknowledgements from Jonny Ross

In writing this book, I am overwhelmed with gratitude for the people who have been instrumental in my journey. Without their support, encouragement and wisdom, I wouldn't be where I am today. From the bottom of my heart, thank you.

First and foremost, to my wife, Lottë, and my children: you are my anchor, my joy and my greatest supporters. My family – mum, dad, and siblings – have always been my backbone, offering opportunities, unconditional love and countless moments of happiness. Your unwavering belief in me has made all the difference.

Oliver Corrigan, one of my first and most enduring clients, your constant inspiration and challenges have shaped my professional journey in profound ways. To Victoria Tomlinson, your guidance in helping me articulate my story and introducing me to the vast world of B2B has been invaluable.

David Bain, your prowess in podcasting and our weekly digital marketing sessions transitioned my focus from blogging to podcasting, opening new avenues for me to share knowledge. Thank you for making me feel at home behind the microphone.

Adam Chandler, our early days of video production and our fun trips to Birmingham will always be cherished memories. To Helen Robinson, Tina Ruddy and Caroline Joynson, your faith in me and strategic insights propelled me forward, allowing me to flourish.

Katy Stuart, your extensive knowledge, dedication and capability have powered my agency, making it what it is today. To James Fry, Adrian Douglas, Neil Preston, Stuart Ramsey and Simon Palmer, thank you for helping me understand my financials and numbers, a critical aspect of running a successful business.

Justin Phillips, Leona Crawford, Phil Fraser, John Kirton, Zaria Pinchbeck, Ben Fox, Al Fox, Andy Fox, Sam Raife and Adam Roney, your belief in me and your role as marketing champions has kept my marketing game strong and opened countless doors.

James Webster, you introduced me to the power of the Internet by creating my first commercial website in 1998, setting the foundation for my digital journey.

Geoff Shepherd, Stuart Clarke, Paul Simpson, Peter Cruikshanks, Martin Port, Elliot Landy, Jane Clynes, Colin Glass, Dr. Simon Jones, Matthew Stroh, Amanda Selvaratnam, Carmel Harrison and David Parkin, thank you for expanding my network, offering speaking opportunities, and providing challenges that spurred growth.

Nigel Glendinning, Jonathan Straight, Dominic Colenso, Daniel Lee, Emma King and Roger Masterson, your inspiration and willingness to bounce ideas have been crucial to my development.

Nigel Cliffe and Steve Phillips, not just fellow speakers but also inspirations. Steve, your resilience in the face of unimaginable personal circumstances continues to inspire me deeply.

Bob Sakayama, the best SEO expert I know, you opened my world to SEO back in 2005. Danny Brown, you affirmed my marketing insights and opinions, giving me confidence in my approach.

Michael Hartley, a passionate and skilled psychotherapist, your influence has extended beyond business strategy, significantly impacting my personal relationships and professional interactions.

To those I have lost, including my grandparents and Richard Cohen, this book is also dedicated to you. Your memories inspire me every day.

Each one of you has played a significant role in my journey, showing me what's possible, opening doors, challenging me, and teaching me. You have all contributed to making me who I am today. Thank you.

Gratitude and Acknowledgements from Pascal Fintoni

This section feels the hardest to write somehow, so I will let myself be guided by looking back at my personal and professional life, and I apologise in advance for anyone that may be missing from this list. I would like to thank the following people.

Let's start with my family, in particular my dad for bringing home our very first home computer, the much beloved Oric Atmos, my siblings for the many years of fun we had learning computer programming and arguing over video games, and my mother for being so forgiving when the telephone bill skyrocketed after too many hours spent on the Minitel.

Next, a very special thank you message to my wife, Denise, for her endless encouragement and for her unwavering belief in me. I am not sure whether you knew you were marrying a dreamer but your support and love makes everything feel possible.

All my 'breakthrough instigators', as I call them, from my first marketing boss Andy Tidy to other equally impressive professionals: Paul Cowley, Sarah Moy, Ingrid Henderson, Joe Murray, Leon Howe, Simon Goon, Suzanne McCreedy, Nicki Clarke and in particular Norma Foster, who so wisely encouraged me to transition from digital marketing practitioner to advisor – thank you to you all.

My brother from another mother, Chris Ducker, for the decades of friendship and constant laughter; you and your family are an inspiration in life and in work. We feel so blessed for knowing you. From the bustling streets of Hong Kong to the green hills of Cambridgeshire, you know I'll always be here for you. Doh jeh sai!

My two amigos, Richard Tubb and Roger Edwards, who keep the flame of content marketing and storytelling truly alive; tracking your own journeys and the amazing contributions you've made to mine has been an experience I will always cherish. Long may it continue!

To Simon Raybould, Clare Josa, Kate MacKay, Beth Hewitt, Simon Clayton, and fellow book authors who showed me the way: thank you for your generosity and patience as I navigated my way through this new territory.

To my accomplices, working tirelessly to make the world of digital more practical, more ethical and more enjoyable, your remarkable influence is beyond measure: Natalie Eminae, Tim Orton, James Mellor, Paul Stainthorpe, Joanne Dolezal, Laura Pearman, Gudrun Lauret, Leanne Miller, Ian Anderson Gray, Ian Farrar, Steve McCormick, Nicole Osborne, Marek Tokarski, Nevil Tynemouth, Tiana Wilson-Buys, Amy Woods, Mark Asquith, the teams at We Are UMi, Business Durham, NBSL, Durham University, Teesside University, and so many others.

And finally, to all my trainees, coaching clients, anyone who has taken the time to participate in my virtual and in-person events, listen to my podcasts series, watch my videos, and read anything I might have written for the print and digital media. Your curiosity and genuine desire to craft a positive online experience and, by extension, craft a better Internet has led to where I am today. Thank you.

Everyone, there are simply no words to express fully how grateful I am for your support and how much you have inspired me.

Pascal Fintoni

Resources for Your Continued Success

Congratulations on reaching the end of *WebProud: The 5-Step Roadmap to Feeling Proud of your Website Again!* Your journey to web mastery doesn't have to stop here.

As a reminder, we have designed and curated a range of additional resources and tools to help you continue transforming your digital presence and achieving outstanding results.

90-Day Website Mastery Programme

Transform your digital marketing in just 90 days! This programme, facilitated by us, Jonny Ross and Pascal Fintoni, is ideal for marketing and sales professionals across all industries.

- **Boost Sales**: Optimise your website for better lead generation.
- **Gain Confidence**: Master the latest digital marketing strategies.
- **Clarity and Action**: Learn where to start and how to measure success.

This dedicated programme includes expert-led training, 1-1 coaching sessions, practical tools, and access to exclusive templates, e-books and private podcast series. Everything you need to feel proud of your website again! https://90daymarketingmastery.com/

Interactive 'Roll the Dice' Tool

Need more inspiration to improve your website? Do you have some spare time for one simple adjustment? Roll the dice to discover one actionable tip and watch a corresponding video to implement it today, thanks to the 'Website Action Randomiser'.
https://90daymarketingmastery.com/roll-the-dice/

The ULTIMATE Website Toolkit E-Book

Discover 50 handpicked tools to help you feel proud of your website again. This e-book provides tech and apps we've personally selected, all designed to simplify tasks, improve performance, and speed up content creation. https://90daymarketingmastery.com/e-book/

The Official Companion to the 90-Day Website Mastery Programme

Stay updated with the latest in digital marketing by tuning in to our podcast, available in both audio and video formats. We wanted to find a way to continue sharing more advice and insights about making your website work harder and for you to feel proud of your website again. Gain insights from industry experts, learn new strategies, and get inspired by success stories.

Video: https://90daymarketingmastery.com/video-podcast/

Audio: https://90daymarketingmastery.com/podcast/

All these resources are designed to provide ongoing support and inspiration as you continue to enhance your website and digital marketing efforts.

Dive in and take advantage of everything we have to offer to ensure your continued success.

Time to feel proud of your website again! Time to be 'WebProud'!

Jonny and Pascal

About The Authors

Jonny Ross

Fractional CMO, Founder of Fleek Marketing and Podcaster

https://jonnyross.com
https://fleek.marketing
https://www.linkedin.com/in/jonnyross/

Jonny Ross is an experienced marketing expert and co-author of '*WebProud': The 5 Step Roadmap to Feeling Proud of Your Website Again!*, dedicated to helping businesses thrive in the digital landscape. As the founder and digital marketing specialist at Fleek Marketing, an award-winning agency, Jonny has built a reputation for driving impactful SEO, user experience and digital marketing strategies. Fleek Marketing collaborates with a diverse range of B2B and B2C businesses, as well as public and third-sector organisations, to enhance their online presence and growth.

With over 27 years of experience in small business and more than 25 years in digital online technologies, Jonny brings unparalleled expertise to his clients. His journey began with running a successful e-commerce business, where he learned firsthand the challenges and intricacies of achieving high Google rankings and effective marketing. This experience fuels his passion for helping businesses navigate the digital world and reach their full potential.

At Fleek Marketing, Jonny focuses on crafting clear, compelling stories that resonate with target audiences. He believes that customers want to be the heroes of their own stories and that businesses should highlight how their products and services can make their customers' lives better. Jonny's approach is client-centric, avoiding marketing jargon and emphasising straightforward, powerful messaging.

Jonny's consultancy work extends beyond Fleek Marketing. He is a sought-after coach, trainer, and public speaker, known for delivering high-standard workshops and training sessions through programmes such as the Natwest Accelerator, Santander Work Café, and the AD:Venture programme for the LEP. His collaborations with institutions like the University of York and Leeds Trinity University underscore his dedication to education and digital skills development.

In 'WebProud', Jonny distills his extensive knowledge into practical strategies, guiding business owners, marketers and entrepreneurs in creating professional, high-performing websites. The book is a testament to his commitment to making digital marketing accessible and effective for all.

Outside of his professional life, Jonny enjoys spending time with his family, camping, and exploring the world we live in. A fun fact about Jonny: he's interviewed Jimmy Corkhill from *Brookside* and appeared on the *Wide-Awake Club* with Timmy Mallett!

Jonny, from Liverpool originally, now lives in Leeds, UK, with his wife and five children. His approachable manner, strategic thinking and passion for helping businesses succeed make him a trusted advisor in the digital marketing community.

Pascal Fintoni

Managing Director, Arclight Marketing and Media Ltd
Senior Digital and Leadership Skills Consultant

www.pascalfintoni.com
https://www.linkedin.com/in/pascalfintoni/

Pascal Fintoni's career path reflects the rise of digital marketing itself. His journey began in the late 1990s, working for a prominent holiday company where he honed his skills in creating multi-channel marketing campaigns across TV, radio, print, and the then-nascent Internet.

In the early 2000s, Pascal made a pivotal transition from digital marketing practitioner to trainer, pioneering his signature course 'How To Get More Enquiries From Your Website'. This shift marked the beginning of his mission to demystify digital technologies for business owners and decision-makers.

This was followed by an invitation from the UK government to lead national and international digital transformation funded programmes, empowering small businesses to embrace new online practices and website solutions.

As a video producer, Pascal has innovatively incorporated storytelling techniques from filmmaking into his coaching methodology, empowering clients to build compelling online reputations. This unique approach, combined with his jargon-free teaching style, has made him a sought-after speaker at conferences and a valued consultant for one-on-one interactive sessions.

Today, Pascal divides his time between public speaking engagements, delivering interactive training sessions, and hosting several podcast series. His ability to translate complex digital concepts, including artificial intelligence, into practical advice has earned him a loyal following among business owners and teams alike.

Pascal's commitment to staying at the forefront of digital innovation is evident in his long-standing work as a podcaster and his comprehensive reviews of over 500 apps and AI solutions designed to enhance business operations.

As the Managing Director of Arclight Marketing and Media Ltd and a Senior Digital and Leadership Skills Consultant, Pascal continues to guide businesses through the complexities of the digital world, helping them harness the power of technology to build successful, proud websites, and proud enterprises.

His first book ' *"WebProud',* is a culmination of his dedication to helping businesses thrive in the digital age.

Printed in Great Britain
by Amazon

54544945R00145